# Who Killed Stutz Bearcat?

*Stories of Finding Faith after Loss*

Kristen Johnson Ingram

Resource Publications, Inc.
San Jose, California

Editorial director: Kenneth Guentert
Managing editor: Elizabeth J. Asborno

Reprint Department
Resource Publications, Inc.
160 E. Virginia Street #290
San Jose, CA 95112-5876

**Library of Congress Cataloging in Publication Data**
Ingram, Kristen Johnson.
    Who killed Stutz Bearcat? : stories of finding faith after loss /
Kristen Johnson Ingram.
        p.        cm.
    ISBN 0-89390-264-0 : $8.95
    1. Ingram, Kristen Johnson.  2. Spiritual life—Catholic
authors.  3. Resurrection.  I. Title.
BX2350.2.I54   1993
248.8'6—dc 20                                                                  93-23775

Printed in the United States of America.

97 96 95 94 93 | 5 4 3 2 1

*Scripture quotations marked RSV are from the Revised Standard Version of the Bible, copyright 1946, 1952, 1971 by the Division of Christian Education o f the National Council of the Churches of Christ in the USA, and used by permission. All other Scripture quotations are from the King James Version of the Bible.*

*Portions of "Children of Grief" appeared in* St. Anthony Messenger *(April 1986); portions of "The Pomegranate Seeds" appeared in* Daughters of Sarah *(May 1990); portions of "Which Passeth All Understanding" appeared in* Daughters of Sarah *(January 1991); portions of "That Spring Should Vanish" appeared in* Arizona Highways *(June 1993); portions of "The Beginning of Wisdom" appeared in* Daughters of Sarah *(Spring 1992).*

*The hymn "Humbly I Adore Thee," appearing in the story "Between Betrayal and Glory," is attributed to St. Thomas Aquinas, translation from* The Episcopal Hymnal 1982 *(© 1982 Episcopal Hymnal Society, 815 2nd Avenue, New York, New York 10017.)*

*For Ron*

# Contents

# Prologue

Death is everywhere. Every experience, good or bad, has the element of death within it: a head of lettuce dies for my dinner salad, an old administration dies when a new President is elected, an artist has to allow the death of five ideas in order to paint the picture of one. In relationships, something or someone is dying all the time— aggression is put to death for the sake of civilization and love is sometimes killed by men and women who do not love enough.

But, to paraphrase St. Paul, where death abounds there resurrection abounds. When the grain of wheat falls into the ground and dies, a new blade springs up; the death of Self means the birth of God within us; children who succumb to cancer will be raised on a final day of glory; and a man like Stutz Bearcat loses his life so that one named Richard can live forever.

# I.
# Children of Grief

*The death of a child, and his friend's resurrection*

When my grandson Andrew was three and a half, his best friend died of cancer.

Mark, who had immense brown eyes and an increasingly tired little heart-shaped face, was two when doctors first assumed the presence of, and found, a malignant tumor bobbing atop his kidney; it grew in him the way an American Beauty rose nudges the skin of its parent plant and buds and bursts open, red as dawn. Cancer cells rushed together like a mob bent on lynching; they grouped and drifted and clung together around Mark's kidney and tried to kill their little host.

"We think we've got it all," the doctors said after the surgery, smiling. Their smiles quieted as they added, "Of course, in these cases, it's hard to say..." and their voices trailed away and they looked off at nothing.

Between chemotherapy treatments, Mark and Andrew learned to pedal their trikes and to use the bathroom; they fought over trucks and Legos sometimes and sang "Jesus Loves Me" at Sunday school. Mark's hair fell out and his skin turned to vellum; he threw up his food. His older brother became waspish and troublesome at school, and his father began to get a reputation among his colleagues for shortness. Mark's mother was never short or waspish but rage quivered just beneath her lips and heaved in the hollow of her throat.

But after Mark quit throwing up and he began to look more like a rosy child, his mother began leaving the boys with her mother or a friend sometimes, so that she could buy groceries or have her hair cut. ("My hair cut!" she kept saying to herself as she listened to the scissors behind her ears. "What if, while I'm here, while they're blow-drying my hair, Something should happen? What if he should...")

But Mark got to be three and the doctors explored his body again, to be sure; and they pronounced him well. "He's clean," they said, as if Mark were freshly healed of leprosy. Churches and prayer groups and women's Bible studies and men's clubs that had been praying for Mark all fell to their knees in thanksgiving, praising God for curing, healing, inspiring doctors, or for casting out the demon of cancer, depending on where they stood theologically. Mark's parents hired a sitter and left for a weekend alone, and their friends hugged one another, crying, "Mark is well! He's well!"

They were wrong. Mark was soon very sick indeed, and doctors fed him platinum and Cytoxin, trying to give him enough poison to kill the cancer without finishing him off. They irradiated him, they cobalted him, they cut his body to ribbons. They failed: cancer after cancer invaded cell after cell, organ after organ. His face turned yellow and his stomach distended; and finally, his parents cried, "No more!" and took him home to die.

Mark's fourth birthday would have fallen the week after Christmas, but just before Thanksgiving his parents had a birthday cake for him. Andrew took him a book and a plastic truck. Mark had quit eating, but his mother spooned a little warm milk into him as Andrew and another child and Mark's brother silently ate their cake and ice cream.

Mark's parents hated putting him to bed, or sleeping themselves, each bedtime a small death to them. His mother held him on her lap as he slept, stroking his sharp-boned little back and rubbing her mouth against his dark hair; she had no tears, only stony anger and cold fear. Mark's father took to getting up in the middle of the night to look at his son and sometimes the older boy, almost ten and blond like his dad, riddled with grief and confusion, woke up too and came out. They would stand by the sick boy's crib and look at him and cry and hold onto each others' hands for wordless comfort.

Mark died the day after Thanksgiving. At the funeral his parents and his brother and his aged, broken grandparents sat in the front row of the church while their weeping friends slipped into the pews behind them; the priest put his hand on the tiny silver coffin and choked his way through the Mass of the Angels.

During the Eucharist, Mark's mother, who had taken plenty of time to have her hair cut and curled and blown dry, looked at her hands and at the floor and at the new stained-glass window, never once letting her eyes fall on the coffin or the altar or the Cross. She never looked into the face of her best friend, my daughter, Andrew's mother, never whispered how ironic it was that she and her husband were godparents to Andrew's healthy little brother.

Afterward she followed the coffin out, leading the older boy, asking that *nobody* come to the graveside, or bring food, or send plants or flowers to the house. While they were at the cemetery some of us sneaked meat loaves and potato salads and cupcakes onto their front deck and then we dashed away, afraid we might incur Mark's mother's hot wrath; we knew it might come forth pitiless, breaking everything in its path; we knew she might come home and shriek, "I said no food!" and throw us off the cliff behind their fence.

On the way home I made a fist and pounded the seat beside me, screaming to God, *You're everything I was afraid you might be, a monster, a villain, who made us for your sadistic pleasure; You're a giant maw, a sucking mouth that consumes us, snatches up and devours a baby on the brink of childhood, licking your divine lips. You're always looking for something to lap up—a deer impaled on barbed wire, a frail pink orchard beaten to death by hail, a child not quite four to be gobbled by cancer.*

And then we told Andrew Mark was gone.

"*Kids don't die,*" he shrieked. He ran about the room, howling like a crazed dog, snapping and snarling at us when we reached for him; every now and then he stopped to fix his mother or father with a wild eye and cry again, "Kids don't die. Only real old people die. Kids *can't* die."

We reminded him how sick Mark had been at the birthday party; all of us weeping, we recalled telling Andrew, "Mark won't get well, honey."

"But kids don't die," he yelled again, and his agony was cosmic. If there is grief in the universe for

the dying of stars, Andrew's lament echoed it. He
called up humanity's most awful fear: *abscondit deus?*
Has God abandoned us? And if so, can kids die?

He ran and yelled until he fell in a heap against
his father.

"Mom told me that when I was an old man—an
old, old, old, *old* man—Jesus would come and get
me," he said, his eyes glazed with sorrow. "But kids
don't die, do they, Dad?" And my son-in-law picked
him up and held him against his chest, unable to
answer.

Soon Andrew's toys began to die. His brown
velvet kangaroo, the corduroy Piglet I had made for
him, his white polar bear—all died and were cast into
graves under his bed. We tried to resurrect them, to
place them on their shelves, but he said they were all
dead and he couldn't play with them.

In a rage that the perfect moment of Andrew's joy
should be pierced by grief, I crawled under the bunk
beds and retrieved the polar bear. "It's not dead," I
said. "Look, Andrew"; and I breathed into the bear's
mouth and gave it CPR and pronounced it living.
*Talitha cumi!* Little girl, arise!

But Andrew threw the resuscitated toy on the
floor.

"Mark is with God," we explained.

"Then I don't love God," Andrew said. "God is
mean and I hate God."

*I know, I know,* I thought, and shook my fist at
heaven.

After a while Andrew's toys quit dying, but he
was wooed by thoughts of death. He would come
into a room where we were cracking filberts or
drinking tea or playing bridge, and say, "I'm dead,"
and slither to the floor in a caricature of death, a

Giaconda smile on his face, his body motionless; and he would lie there till we recognized his condition. "Yes, you're dead," we'd say, or, "No, Andrew, you're not dead," depending on the time of day or the mood we were in.

He got to be four, and four and a half; a year had passed since Mark had fallen asleep in his mother's arms and died, but still Death preyed like a vulture on Andrew's spirit. We convinced him that Mark was with Jesus, and that was a good and perfect state.

"All right," he said, "if it's so good, why don't I die and go there too? Why be alive if it's more fun to be dead?"

Then we gripped the arms of our chairs: could he be one of the horrifying numbers of young children who killed themselves? And why in hell *are* people alive, if it's more fun to be dead?

*Please, God, no,* we prayed, and we talked to Andrew about butterflies and bunnies and built wooden block cities with him until he seemed to forget death awhile.

And then one day my daughter called; Andrew was terribly upset, could I come over? I found them all crying: Andrew was on his top bunk, weeping with terror, his mother was crying with grief for him, and two-year-old Adam was sobbing because everyone else was crying.

"He's afraid," my daughter whispered. "He's afraid he'll die."

*So am I,* I thought, as I climbed up the bunk ladder to Andrew, who was hurling toys and shoes. I dodged several missiles and said, "Come with me."

"Where?"

I thought fast. "To the ice cream store," I said. "We'll get some ice cream."

8

Still sobbing, he backed down the ladder after me
and suffered to take my hand. As I buckled his safety
belt he sniffled and said (*O God!*), "Gra'mother?
Wouldn't it be neat if when people died they came
alive again?"

*What was that sudden increase of light?* I didn't even
notice, then, that the sun and moon were standing
still. I went to the front seat and buckled my own belt
and began backing out the driveway.

"Andrew, somebody did that once," I said,
looking into my side mirror.

"Did what?"

"Came alive after they died." I pulled into the
street. I drove a block and turned right.

"You mean Jesus," Andrew said.

"Yes, Jesus came alive." I glided into the left lane.

After another short burst of silence, he said,
"Well, maybe Jesus came alive, but it didn't help
Mark. What about Mark and me and Mom and Dad
and the baby and the dog and everybody?"

I stopped in the left turn lane and looked into my
rear-view mirror. I could see his smooth-skinned,
blue-eyed face, and he could see me.

"Andrew," I said, "Andrew!"

"What?"

"Andrew, Jesus fixed it so when we die, we'll all
come alive again, too. We call it the resurrection.
Some day, everybody dead will stand up and, well,
be alive."

I made my left turn.

"Really?" His voice was filled with awe.
"Everybody?"

*Each one dies once, and then the judgment.*

"Yes," I said.

"Do you mean *alive*, or just sort of in heaven like a ghost or something?"

"No, I mean alive," I said, parking in front of the Dairy Queen. I unbuckled my seat belt and started to get out, when Andrew's voice caught my heart and broke it.

"Gra'mother?" he said, small and quiet. "Gra'mother, is this like Santa Claus?"

I was chilled, vexed, overwhelmed, shocked, sorrowful, and frozen with terror.

"What do you mean, 'like Santa Claus'?"

"You know. A story you tell little kids."

Sweat beaded up on my forehead and upper lip, sweat like clots of blood. My faith was on its mettle, now: *Was* the resurrection like Santa Claus or the tooth fairy, a story you tell dumb, believing little kids? Did I tell the Jesus story as an ointment to sweeten the air of death and corruption?

"I know that my redeemer liveth," I said.

"What?" Andrew said.

"And that he shall stand in the latter day upon the earth," I said.

"Wha-at?"

"And though worms destroy this body, yet in my flesh shall I see God," I said, louder and clearer, my heart thrumming. *For now is Christ risen from the dead, the firstfruits of those who sleep—*

"What, Gra'mother?"

The sun and moon, motionless above us, brightened the dashboard of my car until my eyes watered. I leapt from the car and opened the back door. My fingers flew over Andrew's seat belt and I grabbed him up in my arms, long and heavy as he was at nearly five, and I cried, "No, Andrew, it's not like Santa Claus. It's true and I believe it."

10

*The light had grown so great that I searched the sky for a comet or fireball or Christ returning.* I set Andrew's feet on the parking-lot asphalt.

"It's true?"

"It's true. Someday Jesus will come back and we'll all be alive again and live forever."

Andrew's eyes contained all the light in the universe. His eye was single and his whole body was full of light. "Really, Gra'mother? Jesus did this?"

"Yes."

"Boy," he said. "Boy. Boy, do I love him, then," he said, joy spilling out of him. "Boy, do I love him for that."

*It was late winter, but the light pummeled at the trees until they budded. The air was rife with the fragrance of life, real life on earth, and not just sort of in heaven like a ghost or something.*

And we went inside, and ate all the ice cream in the world. And death had no dominion.

## For Reflection

Everyday the television shows us the deaths of children: they die from starvation in Sudan, Somalia, and Etruria; from the effects of wars in South America, Africa and Bosnia; in disasters like the burning of the cult home in Waco, Texas, and in hospitals where doctors haven't found cures for the diseases that ravage children's bodies. Consider your response to these deaths: Do they make you angry, or sorrowful? Do they impel you to action? Can you stop the death of one child, anywhere? If so, make a plan for what you'll do.

## For Faith-Sharing

Talk about the meaning of the author's words to her grandson (well-known to lovers of Handel's *Messiah*):

> I know that my redeemer liveth, and that he shall stand on the latter day upon the earth; and though worms destroy this body, yet shall I see God in my flesh (Jb 19:25-26).

as well as the italicized words that followed:

> For now is Christ risen from the dead, the firstfruits of them that sleep (1 Cor 15:20).

## Prayer

> *God, I don't understand the deaths of children. I think I never will, so long as I live on earth. When a child dies I feel resentful and angry. But help me to keep my faith in the Resurrection, and give me compassion always for children who grieve. Amen.*

## Journaling Idea

Write a letter to a young child, real or imaginary, who has lost his or her best friend. Offer this letter up to God by lighting a candle, then burning it in the flames and praying for children who are in any kind of sorrow or trouble.

# II.
# Patty and the Bomb

*Resurrection in violence*

Andrew's first brush with death came when he was only three and a half. I was fourteen before it happened to me.

Oh, I knew people died. Ruthie's daddy, who was always sick, died when we were five. Paul Strengell's daddy, who had coughed for all my six years, died of silicosis of the lungs because he had worked in the mines. Margie Gronlund's dad, a huge man who listed from side to side when he walked, and who was subject to constant nosebleeds, died when I was eight and she ten. But those were fathers, men who had been sick a long time. Someone else's father might pass on but I felt safe, until I was fourteen.

I went to church alone one summer Sunday morning and slipped into a pew beside a girl named Doreen.

"Didja hear Patty Meany died?" she whispered.

*Kids don't die!*

"She died? Patty *died*? Was there an accident?"

Doreen liked to snap her chewing gum, and it cracked on every word as she whispered, "No, she had sugar diabetes and they didn't know it until she got into a comma and died."

*You mean a coma,* I thought, and I wondered why Doreen's mother let her chew gum on Sunday morning; my folks said the sweet juice broke the pre-Communion fast. Maybe Doreen saved old gum for Sunday morning, gum with the juices all gone. I tried to think about Doreen's gum chewing; I tried not to hear what she was saying.

"So Patty won't be back to school this year," Doreen said, snapping the wad of gum. She had a low forehead and wavy black hair that sprang from a widow's peak that nearly intersected her eyebrows. I had been shower partners in gym with her for the whole last year at school: I knew she didn't shave her armpits or use deodorant, and I thought that was the reason I suddenly felt so weak. The warmth of Doreen's undeodorized body surrounded me like an aureole, that was it; the perfume of her arms and legs and throat were suffocating me, and I fainted and struck my head on a kneeler. I lay on a couch in the parish hall until the Mass was over and the priest could drive me home.

Doreen sat on a chair in the parish hall to keep me company.

"Patty's mom tried to call you before she left town," she said.

"Left? Left for where?"

Mrs. Meany was a widow about thirty-five, a kind, humorous woman with thick glasses and apparently of modest means, as she and Patty lived in a tiny, plain apartment. They both liked me and had me for teas and dinners.

Thirty or so pounds overweight, Patty was soft and dark, with a beauty mark near the corner of her mouth. We studied together and sometimes we took the Red Electric to downtown Los Angeles or Hollywood, to a movie.

We talked often about weight: I was always too thin and she too fat, I wanted big breasts and she wanted a flat chest, but we skirted those facts and talked about diets and hormones. At fourteen, Patty had only had two periods, each more than a year apart; her mother was certain that this was the cause of her overweight, and that as soon as Patty's female system got straightened out, she would grow miraculously thin and stylish. I nodded; I had menstruated at ten, and I wondered if that's why I was all angles and long bones, but my mother said it was Swedes in my woodpile.

Patty should have seen an endocrinologist; she went for a yearly checkup at a pediatrician's, just as she still went to have a picture taken at a photographer's in Eagle Rock—sometimes I went with them—but her checkup was sketchy and the pediatrician an old man hustled out of retirement because all the doctors had been drafted.

Earlier that summer, just after school was out, Patty and her mother had ridden the city bus to my house for a tea-party; I remember making an iced cookie loaf that had to be sliced diagonally. They invited my mother and me to their house the next week, but we were going away on vacation; and now that we were back, Patty was dead, and her mother gone.

"Mrs. Meany packed up and left town," Doreen said. "She went to live with relatives in Wyoming or somewhere."

"But the funeral," I said through dry lips. I felt like something hung on a clothesline in freezing weather, stiff and hard in the winds of God.

"There wasn't any funeral," Doreen said. "Her mom had her burned up."

I saw Patty on the ash heap or stuffed into a cement incinerator like the one in my back yard; I saw her arms and legs turn to flame and rise like the limbs of a marionette in the heat; I saw her mother dancing around the flames, a virago screaming, "Burn her up! She's dead and I don't want her."

"You mean cremated," I said.

"Yeah," Doreen said, snapping her gum; and then the priest came and because I had ridden to church on the bus and my parents were gone for the day, he drove me home. He was old and kindly; it never occurred to me to tell him my friend had died, to ask for his counsel or comfort.

My house was empty, my mother and father gone miles and miles through the worst scenery in Los Angeles county to see my uncle in Baldwin Park. I didn't call my uncle's house and blubber out my sorrow; the call was long distance, and it was wartime. We had bitten the bullet for four years now; we were used to going without butter and meat and coffee and gasoline and long distance. My parents had saved their gas rationing coupons a long time to make a trip like the one to Baldwin Park.

I lay on the living room sofa all day, trying to undo Pat's death. Every now and then I would jump up and go to the telephone, but I didn't dial the number. When I finally mustered up the nerve, I wondered what would happen if I heard Patty's voice saying hello, heard her soft, intellectual chuckle. Would I faint again or even die?

16

But what I heard when I finally did dial was an operator, informing me that the number was disconnected.

Late that afternoon, when it was almost time for the church youth group, I staggered up our hill, through a vacant commercial lot and across La Tijera boulevard, to my best friend's house. I had always liked Shirley a little more than Patty, and guilt for that squirted up in my shoes as if I had marched through a deep puddle. I kept seeing Patty's wide, soft face; I could see the space between her teeth; I recalled her glasses sliding down on her low-bridged button nose; I saw her small, rosy mouth and the beauty mark; and I felt guilty because I had always liked Shirley better.

Shirley hadn't been at church that morning, didn't know, and when she opened the door I fell into her carpeted living room and wept. We walked to the bus together crying; we had both loved Patty, but not enough to keep her alive.

All that summer Patty's death surrounded me. I went to the beach every day on the red bus, with Shirley or the youth group; sometimes I rode with the boy down the street who liked to drive people around in his metallic green car, a car like an iridescent June bug. Patty's image rode with me, nodding and smiling, and my chest was heavy all the time.

We all sat on the beach dazzled by the sun and worshiped it with our bodies, letting it feast on our bare backs and limbs and faces except for our noses, ceremonially whitened with thick zinc oxide. Light danced on the ocean and on the chrome of cars and on the windows of hamburger stands; and the god or goddess of light apparently found my fair-skinned

Scandinavian body to be a reasonable, holy, and living sacrifice, because I was nearly consumed by burning.

I blistered and peeled and threw up and broke out in rashes; and when I was well I went back to the beach and lay there again in my modest white bathing suit, telling myself that this time I would turn creamy brown like Shirley. And as I lay there, I grieved for Patty, sometimes inadvertently groaning aloud. Sometimes I accidentally cried; and I remembered Patty had been fair-skinned, too—Black Scot, she said—but she'd had enough sense to stay out of the sun.

I came home from the beach one afternoon in early August, came in the metallic green car and mounted our cement porch dripping sand; and I stooped to pick up the *Los Angeles Mirror* off the step.

"A-BOMB ON JAPS," the black, square letters screamed against their peach-colored wartime paper.

A great bubble of light surrounded me; I felt the worst sunburn of my life eating through my skin and flesh and bone, turning me to lead and then ash and then a silhouette on the gray cement porch. Cloud after cloud of horror rose over me as I walked into the house, reading; I was a smart kid, a kid who had skipped grades in school, and I knew words like cyclotron and Fermi and Split the Atom and Einstein. I knew what it meant.

"What does it mean?" asked my mother. She was wearing a navy blue rayon dress with a white organdy collar; her younger brother Tom, whom some took to be my brother, stood nearby as I read; he was wearing army officers' pink pants and a T-shirt, having done what American boys were supposed to do: he went to the army, got a

18

commission, and then got shot and nearly died, but didn't die. Aries, the god of war, wanted blood sacrifices, but some of them sneaked home.

Tom was my hero, twelve years older than I and looking even younger as he roamed our house, his wounds and stitches hidden under his T-shirt and pink pants, telling us how he got shot by a sniper on Okinawa. He stood there as I read, sand falling from the elastic legs of my bathing suit onto our wool carpet, trying to stammer an explanation to my mother about the mystery of the atom. Neither my mother nor Tom was terribly scientific or mathematical by nature, and eventually she became angry at me because she didn't grasp the principle of atom-splitting, and she walked away, saying she hoped it would all be over soon.

Tom said, "How many Japs were killed?"

"They aren't sure," I said, wanting not to talk, wanting to think. I had to fight rising petulance in my voice. "Maybe twenty thousand or so."

"With *one bomb*? Twenty thousand, at one blow?" he exclaimed, and I started to laugh: I had only that spring in my French class read *Sept-d'un-Coup*, or *Seven at One Blow*, the story of the little tailor who killed seven flies but grew the reputation as a great warrior. *Sept-d'un-coup?* Or rather, twenty thousand at one coup? (We didn't know then the real numbers, didn't know that death had undone so many.) Tokyo had been in flames already, thanks to Jimmy Doolittle's daring daylight raids, but this was more like some awful miracle.

I went to the shower and tried to think. I wriggled out of my bathing suit, knowing my father would yell that night about sand in the drain. I washed the seawater out of my long hair and tried to think about the bomb; unless the Japanese were harboring a like weapon, I thought, the war was surely over but the bomb wouldn't be.

Pulling my bathrobe off its hook, I crept out of the bathroom, wrapping my hair in a towel. I left my bathing suit on the floor, and a great ring of sand, but I was overtaken by a terrible fatigue and couldn't clean them up then. I sat on the side of my bed, and tried to call Patty's face up, but she smiled and faded away and the image intruded of a thousand bodies falling on my right hand and ten thousand on my left, people not cremated like Patty but crisped and evaporated in the flames of hell. I could see an atom, much like a round vitamin pill, circling round and round and round in the cyclotron and then suddenly swelling into a new sun, one that would shake the earth forever.

"Now, nothing will ever be the same again, as long as I live," I said out loud. My innocence was gone now; all humanity's innocence was gone. God's created son and daughter had sunk their teeth into the fruit of the tree of the knowledge of good and evil and we were fallen, fallen into the abyss.

"Patty," I said, stretching out on my bed, wincing as my sunburned back touched the hard mattress. "Patty, go to God, now."

Her face hung over my ceiling, wide and gentle-eyed.

"No," I said. My loss was complete, my vows of grief fulfilled. I let Patty begin her journey toward resurrection, while my generation, nearly fifty years ago, became the first to struggle in the shadow of a terrible new Light.

## For Reflection

Somehow, the dropping of the bomb on Hiroshima released the author from her grief for her friend and into another kind of mourning. Which was worse—her grief for Patty, or her horror at the fate of humanity? Think of a time you grieved for someone. Did that process stop suddenly, or did your mourning gradually end?

## For Faith-Sharing

Discuss how you pray at a time of personal grief and what your prayers are during a national disaster. What do you expect of God when death strikes?

## Prayer

> *God, I remember the first time I lost someone to*
> *death. I can still feel the pain of that person's absence,*
> *still feel the shock of that person's dying. Please bless*
> *(name) in the sure hope of the Resurrection. Amen.*

## Journaling Idea

Write the names of all the friends or relatives you have lost to death and the approximate date they died. Pray the above prayer for each one.

# III.
# The Pomegranate Seeds

*The dying earth, and the resurrection*

*Persephone was kidnaped by Pluto, and taken into Hades. While she was there, her mother, Demeter, stalked the earth in a rage and refused to let any grain grow; the earth was barren and laid waste and famine reigned. No matter with what delicacies he plied her, Pluto could not entice Persephone to eat. "I want food from the earth," she said, but no food could be found except one wizened pomegranate. Finally she ate six seeds from the fruit; as a consequence, half the year on earth all plants and living things will die.*

When you appropriate Jesus' mercy over your life, you may realize too late that you'll also be subjected to his opinions about everything else.

And his opinion is, to say the least, polarizing. Jesus isn't one to pussyfoot around like J. Alfred Prufrock; Jesus isn't politic or even careful. If he had been, the story might have turned out rather differently.

It's got to be one way or the other, Jesus says: to wear God's colors means to wear them all the time, and to wear them means to choose the side that is salvific—but also unpopular, abrasive, and prophetic.

If, for instance, I profess belief in the Resurrection, then I have to extend mercy to the people who sleep in green plastic garbage bags under the bridges in my city, who sometimes groan and die, unknown. Because they may be present at the Resurrection, to point their fingers and say. "She passed us by," and I could be cast into outer darkness. Besides: there's something about experiencing the love of God that draws you to the poor and suffering.

And if I renew my life in the earthy facts of Eucharist, I must also take part in my country's decisions about African states. Because *all* bread comes off the Lord's table, because all food is the bread of heaven, then my right to participate in the Communion carries with it the responsibility to see what the rest of the world is eating, and who is holding a gun to whose head.

If I presume on the wild act at Golgotha for my salvation, then I have to work for the poor, the downtrodden, the prisoners, the mourners, and the hungry. I am sucked up into that whirlwind whence heaven speaks and I therefore have to be careful for nothing except what is Christ's.

And without Christ was no thing made, without the Word the galaxies would not shimmer with pulsars and ringed planets and comets and mysterious dense black masses of raw energy; without Christ—without grace—my own planet, suspended somewhere in the dark arch of Creation,

could never have resonated with the cry of water
leaping over its bed of gray rocks or the rasp of trees
flinging dry red leaves into the winds, or of
moist-barked branches moving like fiddle bows over
each other. Christ's is that relentless energy that boils
and spits through the universe and yields up cactus
and crows and zebras and finally men and women
crowned in the very image of their Creator. The earth
is charged with innocence and mercy and
replenishment: the Spirit brooded and danced over
the waters, coaxing them out of chaos.

So if that same Spirit thrums within me, I don't
dare to transform what was naive and playful for
God into a mound of stiff-legged, swollen animals
killed for sport, or occlude the hills with a structure
of convenient plastic diapers and handy styrofoam
cups, or spew yellow-foamed filth into a river that
once made glad the city of God.

So. Every few days I take several rolls of exposed
black-and-white film to a camera store where the
owner, a man who reminds me of an astonished
Kodiak bear, scribbles up my order and subtracts my
professional discount; then he hands over the latest
envelopes full of my photographs.

"A bag for those?" he says every time.

Usually I shake my head and smile; I don't want
his crisp, rustling, pink plastic bags. *Usually* I just
shake my head and smile, trying to balance my
principles about the earth against my principles
about Christian courtesy.

One day, though, I went nakedly mad for a
moment and I cried, "No, no, no! Those bags will lie
in a landfill for three hundred thousand years!"

He gasped and a reddish film slid over his eyes,
either grief or exasperation; I don't know which.

Startled by my own outburst, I paid my bill and fled to sit in my car.

I wondered, out there, not *whether* there is something I could do to save the earth, but whether it is futile to try.

I muttered to myself. "They'll never see the truth," I said. "It's too late. Congress can be bought, the administration won't listen, industry cares only for itself and its lobbies are more powerful than I am, people don't give a damn, for every one of me fighting plastic bags twenty more will prefer them, what difference does one bag make when the paper mill near me is destroying the river, even if someone wanted to do something the money isn't there, the male-originated, male-dominated institutions are inured."

Well, now. Having listened to my own diatribe, I began to argue with myself. Because although the *institutions* that muck up the environment are the possible result of several thousand years of male-generated arrogance for (and domination over) "inferior" things like flowers, topsoil, deer, babies, lap dogs, streams, lakes, women, trees, rabbits and birds, even though the conspicuous spoiling of the land and its creatures probably sprang from that fallenness that Phyllis Trible calls "the sin of Patriarchy"—and even though I would like to affix blame for the wicked wasting of Creation on every man ever born—I have to writhe in guilt, too, because when the shameless light of God's all-seeing eye falls on guilty *individuals*, I am of course among them.

I am among them not so much for things like the see-through zip-top bags I occasionally indulge in, nor even so much for things like ignorance when I was younger that led me to spraying insect killers and fluorocarbons into the air: but I *am* guilty for the word not spoken, for not risking my life for what was right.

Once I would have. Twenty or so years ago I chanted and marched and lay down on federal steps, willing to be spit on, shrieked at, dragged by my thin arms or long hair to the patrol car and then jail, for causes like school integration and the draft and the mining of certain foreign harbors. Now, in middle age, when my arms are heavier and my expensive haircut is short, I preach righteousness while occulting my imperatives to action behind fences of arthritic bones and fatigue, behind editorial deadlines and a feeling of futility...

"That's it!" I cried aloud, sitting in my car, and an Airedale dog in the black Volvo next to me barked reproachfully.

But I'd found not only my guilt, but my guile. Futility is the sin that can give me hideous veined wings and scales and claws. It doesn't gleam like sins of passion or even the failings of ignorance, but it is the evil lapses that occur in moments of despair.

If I pretend that a righteous cause is futile, if I neglect to storm heaven with my prayers, if I murmur, "What's the use?" and fold my hands over my bosom and let my eyes roll up as their lids shut, then I am in danger of unceasing hell fire.

Because I have no right to those lapses. They blaspheme the Spirit dolloped onto me at my baptism. Nothing is futile, nothing; God plus one is a majority and if I take the tiniest first step toward environment's enemies, Christ will seize the battle in the same way that God told the people of Deuteronomy, "Do not fear the peoples of Canaan, for the battle is mine"; if I even *ask* for strength, the

Word that brought the universe into being will also grant me the grace and power to war against the *lavastatus* of the earth.

I drove away from the camera store and went to lie on the grass of my back yard. I could smell the rich, moist soil: its hidden root-and-runner mysteries were like the dark veins in my womb that once nourished babies who would become my children who would become spectacularly beautiful adults. My heart and limbs, formed with the first human's, from the dirt, are therefore plunged in earth like the deep roots of evergreens. I wept that day, and my tears fell between sharp blades of grass; a minuscule, shiny insect dodged and scuttled away into a crack in black soil.

Suddenly I remembered Luise Ranier, a movie actress of my childhood, her features painted and stretched to be vaguely Oriental: I remember her grubbing to plant a peach pit, looking in the soil for roots, even boiling up a pot of dirt and water for her children to eat when China was struck by famine. That movie was *The Good Earth*, from the novel by Pearl Buck. The subject was one woman's connection to the land, and what it yielded; and at the end, when she lay, rich and bedecked and simple on her deathbed, her husband cried, "O Lei-Ping, you are the Earth!"

And at that moment he blessed into action every woman who, having appropriated the grace of Jesus, is now subjected to his ideas about the environment; so I will have to toss futility into the lake of fire, and believe that miracles happen. For who could ever have thought that human beings could fly into space like wild geese, or that what we called the "Iron Curtain" would be torn away like flimsy paper? Who would have thought we could really stamp out smallpox or plague? Who would ever, ever, have thought, that God could become a human being?

The earth was laid to waste when Persephone was a captive in Hades, but the sentence is over. We can participate in Earth's resurrection; we can end the curse and restore the land.

All right. Break forth together into singing, ye waste places of Jerusalem[1]: I can come alive again. I can emerge from my sepulchre of futility to cajole, to coax, to scrap and battle for that ecology chain in which I am linked, to the soil whose dark remembrance cries out in my genes and lies under my fingernails at planting time; whose justice yields the sweet wine and nuts of feasting; whose upper firmament insists on the glory of God. I can brood over the waters and point my finger at dirty streams and dirty politicians; I can beg from the rich and give into the poverty of the land.

I can even pray, saying, *Yes, yes, Lord. All the earth and the fullness thereof.*

### For Reflection

When God gave Adam and Eve dominion over the earth, did God mean we could run roughshod over Creation—or that the buck stops with us? What areas of "earth-murder" bother you most? What everyday conveniences are you willing to give up to save the planet?

---

[1] Isaiah 52:9

## For Faith-Sharing

Talk about the ways Scripture describes our planet and its creation in the first chapter of the Gospel of John. Discuss what the Church's role should be in environmental protection.

## Prayer

> Lord Jesus, you came not to condemn the world but to save the world. Give me the wisdom to be a blessing to this planet, a creator rather than a destroyer, a life-sustainer rather than only a consumer. Wound my conscience when I waste or pollute or ruin something you have made; strengthen me to "fight the good fight" for coming generations who will have to live in what I have left behind me. Amen.

## Journaling Idea

Write down three ways you might take part in resurrecting our planet. Later, journal how you carried out at least one of these plans.

# IV.
# Which Passeth All Understanding

*The death and life of peace*

When I was five years old, I had a tall, slender book called *Wing Wang Wu*. Its water-color pictures, most of them wide-brushed in pink and gray, depicted a young Chinese boy who danced all over the world. I hardly remember the story, but I remember the way his long braid flew as he danced, and I remember the lines,

> He danced through England
> and he danced through Spain...

because every time my mother read it to me during lunch (at which time I twirled around the room, dancing and stuffing a sandwich into my mouth), I would stop whirling to say sadly, "There's war in Spain." She would nod patiently, the way mothers do at their children's rituals, and then we went on. We probably repeated this routine for a month or so, and then I got another favorite book.

I'm not sure I knew what "war" meant when I was five years old; in those gentler days, we didn't have television, we didn't bring battle into our living rooms. But the year after that, when I could read the newspapers and the *Movietone* captions, Japan invaded China, and I knew. I read and I knew.

Two years later, Hitler marched into Poland with the best-organized army ever seen until then. And in another two years, when I was ten, when the United States rose up in shock and horror at the spectacle of Pearl Harbor and entered World War II, I knew what it was about. I scoffed, along with all the other kids gathered around our schoolroom radio, when Congresswoman Jeanette Rankin, saying she could not send young men to be killed, refused alone to vote for war; I cheered when President Roosevelt said that a state of war existed; but beneath my joyful wartime camaraderie, my bowels rumbled with fear.

Some days I could hardly think at school, because the study of war was so consuming. I learned words like "allies" and "atrocities"; I learned to pronounce Luzon, Marianas, Mindanao; I could spit out an execration of Hitler, Tojo, Mussolini, Hirohito, Goebbels, Himmler. My weekly girls' club met after school to prepare for war by marching in squads, to call out commands like, "Quarter wheel to the right, maaa-arch!" At Girl Scouts we knitted kakhi-colored yarn into squares for Red Cross afghans: I usually had to rip my squares out and start again. In fourth-grade history we brought clippings from the newspaper, clippings about Rommel and rationing.

My grandmother leaned over the radio every night, hoping for some scrap of information about her son, my young uncle, in the Pacific Theater of Operations. Her body was tiny and her knuckles arthritic; she clutched her Tweed-scented handkerchief and murmured prayers as she listened, made the news into a litany wherein every bulletin was answered, "Lord, have mercy."

"When I grow up, I'll only have daughters," I told my mother. "Boys get killed."

The boy next door to us went to war and got killed. My mother's younger brother, only ten years older than I, was shot at Okinawa and came home to our house, angry and permanently wounded. By the time I was fourteen and we dropped the bomb on Hiroshima, war was as familiar to me as milk and wool blankets and paperback books.

And my decision that nothing would ever, ever be the same after that bomb was true. My first child was born soon after we entered Korea: I remember holding her in my arms a few months later, and weeping hysterically as the President on television declared a state of national emergency. A couple of years later we were still at war and I was terrified just before the birth of my second child; what if it should be a boy?

While I was pregnant with that second daughter, I awoke one night to what seemed the end of the world. Our little house was shaking and the floors rolling; my daughter's crib was slamming into our bed and she was wailing. I could hear canned goods and glassware crashing to the floor a few rooms away. Suddenly the room was bright, and I nearly swooned with fear. We looked out the window. The sky lit up; it was blinding.

"Get dressed," said my husband. "And dress the baby," and we prepared to live through a hydrogen bombing. What we were actually living through was an earthquake; the lighted sky came from the blowing of transformers at a nearby power plant. But the fear we had gone through filled us with hate for someone we couldn't see. The Russians, the Chinese, *somebody*. We danced through the Cold War like Wing Wang Wu, and we taught our babies never to be out of our sight, or their grandmothers' sight. Ever. We talked about bomb shelters. We used the term "fallout" as easily as we said "salt" or "hello."

Peace broke out—except in Cuba and Hungary and the Suez. "Do you realize," I said to people, "there's a *revolution* going on in the world?" My limbs quivered with delight, for revolutions led to peace and plenty, didn't they? Didn't they? My son was born and I held him in my arms and wept before the television as I saw Hungary swept away, saw a twelve-year-old boy shooting with an ordinary rifle at a behemoth Russian tank. The tank rolled over him like an iron over a plaid skirt, and I pressed my son closer to my body.

During the Cuban Missile Crisis in 1962, the children had air-raid drills every hour or so at school. On Tuesday of that week my little boy came inside covered with dirt.

"Have you been *fighting*?" I cried. My children were forbidden to fight. But no, he'd been on his way home from first grade; passing the local high school as he climbed the hill toward our house, he had heard a bell ring. Thinking it was an air-raid alarm, he jumped into the gutter to "duck and cover."

I yanked the draperies shut and, in a rage, started a pot of water for spaghetti. *They should let the mothers of the world take over*, I thought as I wiped my son's face and hands and elbows with warm water. *They should let the mothers of sons run the governments.*

We elected a President of peace and killed him. By the time my daughters switched their skirts and fluttered their eyelashes over boys, we were sunk deep in the jungle mud of Vietnam and those boy friends were fragile, nervous and vulnerable. They talked about college deferments, of trips to Canada, even about going to prison rather than to war. The flag did not inspire them, nor could the President call their manhood to account: they had watched the war on television every night, and they didn't want to go. And I wept at night, because my son was growing older.

Sometimes our family all marched together, demonstrating, carrying posters, singing John Lennon's words about giving peace an opportunity, or chanting, "I ain't gonna study war no more...." Just after our oldest daughter married an architectural student, college deferments were canceled and the first draft numbers were called. My new son-in-law's draft number was *three*. We offered to drive him to Canada; but his father had been a soldier and he didn't want to shame the family. He hurried into a reserve unit and spent six months in boot camp where he was taught to yell, "Kill, kill kill."

My son turned seventeen and I sucked in my breath, ready for the worst; but we left Vietnam and fell to fighting among ourselves instead. Peace broke out—but only for a moment; we had to remain in Saigon after the armistice, to watch the bloodbath, to study war a few years longer. We turned on our self-centered President and drove him from office, and called up another one who taught us distrust. When we elected a man of God, he was ridiculed and drummed out of the city. We learned to play war with Syria and Lebanon and Iran, to sacrifice a few

Marines here and there so we would look strong. "Powerful Presence" became a buzzline; we invaded safe, soft targets like Grenada and Panama and helped to depopulate other Central American states.

One day I read about a little girl with no hands: the *Contras*, our Powerful Presence in Nicaragua, had pushed her against a wall and used her hands for target practice. The magazine said the Contra soldiers were drunk and singing as they shot the child. Some organization sent the child to the United States for treatment of her handless arms and her mental confusion. She had not spoken since that incident.

Just after I read that gut-twisting piece (in a reputable Christian magazine), I went to lunch at the home of friends. Their other guest was a young soldier they'd met at church, a National Guardsman just back from Honduras, where he'd been sent to guard the border to Nicaragua; he was now returned in triumph.

"You may not understand the war down there," he said, rosy and expansive, important. "See, rebels are trying to overthrow the government of Nicaragua and the Contras, who are the government forces. We was stationed in Honduras and the government Contras had to come in there to reconnoiter from the Communist rebels. The president of Nicaragua,... uh—"

"Ochoa. Daniel Ochoa," I said.

"Yeah, well, he asked for our help in getting rid of the Communist rebels."

I froze into silence. Was this poor boy representative of what was defending our country? A man who apparently hadn't read a newspaper for ten years? Had we all boarded the Ship of Fools?

35

Explaining or arguing would have been whipping a dead horse, but the image of the little girl rose up before me with outstretched bloody stumps; I mumbled that I was sick, and I left the luncheon guilty and afraid. Central American martyrs hissed and whispered in my ears: Cardinal Romero, nuns, lay workers, Jesuits, housekeepers, children.

Sure, we're talking peace everywhere now. Walls have fallen; nations are talking about ploughshares. Governments have fled. But every day I waken to the news and when I hear, "This is Bob Edwards with Morning Edition," I brace myself for the worst. Every evening I look at pictures of that worst: Our Powerful Presence went to the Gulf, which really proved only that mothers of daughters now have to shake in fear, too. Croatians and Serbs, Georgians, Blacks and Whites, Browns and Yellows, all massed at their ramparts, killing and dying. Bloods and Crips, shooting each other even before puberty. I know war now; I eat it with my dinner and breathe it with my morning prayers.

Peace is something we "pass" at church every Sunday, but all I ever knew was war.

I see only one possibility for the resurrection of peace on earth: *Even so, come quickly, Lord Jesus.*

## For Reflection

Try to remember a moment of peace in your life—when no war was raging in the world, when your household was without strife, when you were in harmony with yourself and others. Imagine life being like that all the time. How have you devoted yourself to the causes of peace, within and without? How can you extend those efforts in the future?

## For Faith-Sharing

With at least one other person, locate a war that's going on somewhere right now, and pray for the country(ies) involved. Discuss whether Christians should bear arms, and find New Testament Scripture to support your ideas.

## Prayer

> *In my lifetime, Lord, peace has been something I've known only in snatches and short moments. Make me a peacemaker somewhere—in my home, my work, my community, or at a global level. Let me be your emissary, proclaiming healing for my world. Amen.*

## Journaling Idea

Write down all the wars that have taken place in your lifetime, and those you've heard family members talk about. Now write a "Declaration of Peace" in your own words: for the world, for your family, and for your inner life.

# V.
# The Fifth Circle of Hell

*The resurrection and the death of sin*

It all began one wet Oregon spring with an explosion of arthritis. I squirmed my way through the nights, looking for a spot where I could set my wrist or knee, seeking seconds of rest that wouldn't be shattered by bursts of pain. The daylight hours were no better; my bones felt huge and swollen, red and sore at their junctions, brittle and hollow and perilous. I quit swimming and walking and dancing; I lay down and read magazines and ate cookies, but this was not enough life for me. So finally by midsummer I crept to the doctor, who nodded and hmmed as he felt my joints and poked at my neck; and he sent me home with a purse full of red pills that were virtually guaranteed to free me from pain and inflammation.

They did that. They also ate a hole through my stomach.

After a summer of pangs behind my sternum, a summer during which I visited eight countries, climbed Palatine Hill and the Acropolis and the Via

Dolorosa, a summer full of odd symptoms for which I finally began taking nitroglycerin, I was in late October rushed to the hospital with acute arm and chest pains. The same doctor that gave me the red arthritis pills was now certain I was having a heart attack.

"How long have you had those fat deposits in your eyes?" he asked, leaning over me in ICU.

Fat deposits! In my eyes! I wanted to reach up; I longed to wipe the lard from my lids. No wonder my mascara ran so frequently: my fat eyes were probably melting, sending down a flow of thick juices like those that lie in the bottom of a turkey roaster. Fat eyes, I had fat eyes, and I wondered if I would go blind. Probably. And if they found out I had given myself fat eyes by eating cookies all summer, they would probably even deny me Talking Books and a guide dog.

"Fat deposits?" I asked.

"A thin circle of white at the bottom of the iris. We see it in people who are ripe for heart attacks. Of course, sometimes it's familial."

I craned and stretched, looking around the room to see if I had a mirror near me; but all I could see was my own heart, beating—rather steadily, I thought—on a monitor at the side of the bed. The monitor had a clone up at the nurses' station, along with other exotic telemetry. My body was wired to the world so that anyone could peep, anyone could see me start at a noise or drop into fitful sleep. A dark orange oxygen tank was pumping into my nose and lungs, and I asked the doctor if I were really having a heart attack.

"Get a nap," he said, and called the nurse to shoot more painkillers into my I.V. I slept, and sometime during the night, I realized how tired I was of my life, and I began to die.

In the morning, a doctor in red glasses fluoroscoped my abdomen.

"Just as I thought. There's the little bugger, right there," he said. I looked at the screen and saw a gray mass. Perhaps soon my body would be as dead as my soul.

"Is that a cancer?"

"No, it's your stomach. Now look down here," he cried, excited, smiling. "On the pyloric wall. You've got a great big ulcer, doing its best to perforate. In fact—yep, it's bleeding to beat hell." He turned around and fixed a red-glazed stare of accusation on me.

"You've been having black stools, haven't you?"

I didn't know. I hadn't looked.

After I had drunk enough barium to permanently cement my entrails, I lay quietly, not arguing or even being present to the doctor who took more X-rays. I didn't move while my arm drank two pints of plasma and some incredibly expensive red blood cells. My body went home a few days later with instructions to take four ulcer pills daily and six doses of antacid— but not together; to eat a bland diet; to take massive doses of Vitamin B-12; to rest every day; to desist from the arthritis medicine forever; and to avoid all stress.

"In that case, call the President," I said. "He's driving me crazy." Nobody either laughed or called the President.

I was pasty-skinned and reclusive. Because I was dead I rested more and more, and my friends and family encouraged me.

"You've been pushing too hard," they said. "You've got to think of yourself this time." I don't know what they meant by "this time"; I am by nature self-centered. Sinful. But I obeyed. I thought of myself, and wept at the thought. And I couldn't get well.

Before it was all over, I had lost seven pints of blood, and when the doctor ordered an endoscopy, I assented, not caring what anyone did to me or about me. The endoscopy was horrible enough to wake me briefly from apathy; in fact I swore to myself that when the doctor got that garden hose out of my mouth and esophagus and stomach and duodenum, I would slay him. Apparently he knew that, so he got even ahead of time.

"I'm going to dilate your esophagus," he said. "Squeeze the nurse's hand if you want some Valium, and she'll shoot it into the I.V."

*Squeeze the nurse's hand?* I couldn't move; I was paralyzed with pain and fear. And I felt my throat burst.

But pain and fear, which are symptoms of being alive, went away and then I was dressed and standing in the day surgery waiting room, dead again.

"Boy, you've had a long history of ulcers," the doctor said. "You're scarred like your stomach had chicken pox." I didn't bother to say I knew that; I'd had an ulcer as a baby. "You've got to quit smoking and give up coffee," he said. "And don't take any more aspirin or anti-inflammatories." He didn't tell me how to get my life back. I only smoked two or three cigarettes a day; some days I didn't smoke any, so I didn't quit just then.

My younger daughter got married a month later and I managed to cope, because nobody realized that I was dead, a *golem* in a long green dress. There was an uproar between the groom and his parents, and the parents didn't fly in for the wedding. I drank rum in milk and took Valium to dull the sounds of the uproar, and everyone complimented me on my calm. The groom and my daughter and I had a corollary uproar, and I offered to let them manage their own wedding. But my daughter wept to both of us, and I went on through the motions of wedding preparation—calmly, as a dead person is calm. I even quit taking rum and Valium, because I was too removed to need them.

The groom's sister and her husband occupied the groom's parents' pew. My first husband, who was recovering from open heart surgery, sat with his wife in the pew behind me after he handed our daughter over to her groom. His wife wore a beautiful cranberry chiffon dress. My son-in-law sang "Jesu, Joy of Man's Desiring," and the bridesmaids included my older daughter and my daughter-in-law. My son was the best man. The church was filled, and light poured down on the wedding party from the clerestory windows. At home after the reception, after the bridal party had left, after I had changed out of my green gown and into real clothes again, my first husband's wife got very drunk and shouted hatreds and obscenities at us. My daughter and daughter-in-law both began to cry.

"I'm sick of this f—-ing elegant family," the wife shrieked. "I'm leaving."

"Good," I said, my new dead calm for once useful to everyone. "I'll call you a cab." She rushed out the door and I locked it and called a cab. Apparently it picked her up, because when my former husband got to his hotel she was gone, taking with her his nitroglycerin. I brought him mine, now no longer necessary. I plied him with tranquilizers and we put him on his plane looking almost as serene as I.

But I was not serene; I was in hell, in the fifth circle of hell, in the punishment for what John Ciardi has described as the likely sin of the twentieth century, in what Dante describes as—having left the violence and color of heresy—a place

> of heavier woe; for each star is falling now...Far murkier was the wave than sablest grain; and we in company of the inky waters, journeyed... into a dismal stream.[1]

No fireworks here, no bright, blazing sins; and Dante says through the mouth of Virgil,

> This too for certain know, that underneath the water dwells a multitude, whose sighs into these bubbles make the surface heave, as thine eye tells thee wheresoe'er it turn. Fix'd in the slime, they say, "Sad once were we, in the sweet air made gladsome by the sun, carrying a foul and lazy mist within: Now in these murky settings are we sad." Such dolorous strain the gurgle in their throats, but word distinct can utter none...[2]

*Acedia*, they call it; in some old English books it is *accidie*. Nowadays it is translated "sloth," which brings to mind physical laziness, and is therefore wrong: the torpor is in the spirit.

To be sure, I also became lazy in my body, and ate more cookies, and nearly pushed my sinful soul

---

[1] Ciardi, John, trans. *The Purgatorio of Dante.* New York: Mentor Books, 1957-1961.

[2] Dante. *Hell*, Canto VII.

toward gluttony, perhaps a lesser sin. Acedia is a
great sin, a refusal to confront the eternal, a failure in
both *eros* and *agape*, a refusal to live in "the sweet air
made gladsome by the sun," or for that matter, to live
truly in any air, gladsome or rainy. An Anglican
bishop once called the day of acedia, "The day in
which you would be cynical about everything, if you
had the energy." Doctors are prone to calling it
depression because they do not always detect the
illnesses of the spirit; if they did, they would advise
prayer, but that would be useless because one caught
in the sin of acedia cannot pray.

I lay dead in thick dark mud that oozed up
between my toes and dried there; my brain and spirit
turned to black clay. I was dead through Christmas,
and New Year's, and through an Epiphany party at
my house, one where we brought gifts to the Christ
child. My grandson Andrew was five, and he gave us
a report on a book about wild cats, including "the
Jag-wah." I hardly laughed all that day, though, for
fear I would disturb the stinking mud around me.

But finally as another spring began to erupt
around me, someone confronted me, someone who
wore a liturgical stole over his shoulders.

"What's wrong with you?" he asked.

"I've been sick. I'm tired of being sick all the time."

He sympathized; we talked about God, who
teases and flirts, and whom I was no longer willing to
chase.

"God hates me," I said, and for the first time in
months I began to cry, because I recognized a lie
when I heard one.

"What is it?" he asked. "You're so depressed. Do
you need to rest more?"

"My Lord, no," I said, and I felt the mud beginning to slide away from my eyes and lips. "I need to confess my sins."

And so I told him the story of my red pills and my stomach and the wedding and the long illness. But this time I told the whole truth.

First I told him about the job I had lost early in the summer, soon after I got the red pills, a job that I thought I was doing well, even brilliantly, until I got fired; and I confessed the enemies I hadn't known I had until I was betrayed and fired. I told that I had not prayed once for these enemies, or even cursed them; I had walled hate and despair into a vault in my heart, and pretended not to be angry. I told him I had indulged myself, had pitied myself, had demanded and gotten kindness and sympathy and service, had refused to pray or think or even shake my fist at God. And in all those months, I, the full-time professional writer, had not written one word.

"This is a deadly sin," said the priest, pulling at his stole to even it. "It's called—"

"Acedia," I said, and wept; and he nodded, and absolved me.

The penance he gave me was to say a whole rosary. I dislike saying the rosary; I find no value in it for my spiritual life, but at that point I was not about to argue with the man who was guarding my soul.

It was late night by then; I went to bed and lay there, telling my beads. I thought I would never get through it: each decade stretched out longer and longer, and I tried to pray faster, to do anything I could to complete my penance. They say that if you leave your beads partly unsaid, the angels will finish your prayers; but I didn't think that applied to penances. I slogged through the final decade, and fell asleep with the rosary still wrapped around my hand.

I dreamed that I was on a cruise ship where entertainments were offered on every deck, some in salons, some under outdoor canopies. But I became disaffected and wandered away to the edge of the boat, nearly falling in and drowning before I realized that the wooden deck surface sloped directly into the water. In fact, my purse fell in and disappeared in the dark sea. Worse, worse: my [then] three-year-old grandson Adam had followed me, and was almost slipping into the ocean himself.

Panting, frantic, I managed to put him on my back and began to climb up, scrabbling at the planked floor whose boards turned under my hands like window jalousies. Finally I got to a long, steep, round-and-round corridor with a rail, where Adam got off and we began pulling ourselves upward. The corridor was filled with people, all striving toward the top.

"Did you get a number?" someone asked me.

"A number?" I reached into my blouse pocket and pulled out two cards, one for me and one for Adam. I can almost see those numbers now: I think mine had nines in it, but it eludes me.

People around me looked at the cards and began to nod. "These numbers mean you're going to make it," they said. I started to cry with relief, but that frightened the toddler, so I smiled and kept going all the way to the top.

It was like a scene from the Love Boat. People were embracing and exchanging addresses and throwing kisses to the captain, whose face I can't remember.

"Do you have any identification?" he asked me. "I can't let you off without identification."

O God: my purse was in the sea, lost. And Adam was tugging at my hand.

"I...I lost it," I said. "But in my room down the street, I have a valid United States passport."

"That's good enough," the captain said, and I stepped out onto solid land. A pale yellow building barred the landscape across the street; although I think we were in San Francisco, the building was the San Diego Department of Justice.

I took Adam's hand and we walked along the embarcadero. Adam was singing and laughing and skipping. I was almost awake again, pushing against the membrane of the dream; but then I heard the captain call, "Kris." I turned and looked at him over my shoulder.

"Kris," he said again, "go and sin no more."

I woke in velvety darkness and hugged it to me.

## For Reflection

What a lay person might call "depression" a theologian might sometimes call "sin." People do need help to overcome depression, but those in acedia need the Church's glorious gift of reconciliation. The cure for acedia is prayer, yet it seems to be the thing most repulsive to someone who is in the midst of it. Can a faithful, undeviating prayer life help you stay out of sloth? What other things can you think of that can prevent or heal this state of mind?

## For Faith-Sharing

In a spirit of openness and trust, discuss the times in your own lives when you fell into sloth—even if for only a few hours. Talk about how lack of hope separates us from God and how it can be overcome in the Christian community.

## *Prayer*

> *Some days, I can't pray, can't move, can't even think.*
> *Hod me in the palm of your hand, God, so I don't*
> *topple into the mire of sloth; so infuse me with your*
> *grace that I can do the work and the prayer that is at*
> *hand.*

## *Journaling Idea*

Write all the words you can think of by free association that describe the state of acedia. If possible, pull these words out of your own store of experience. They may include "depression" or "laziness" or even "feeling overwhelmed." You may think of "fatigue" or maybe "passivity." After you have listed these words in a column, write their direct opposites beside them (for example, "joy" beside "depression"). Pick the word you think best describes the spiritual state you want to be in, and then use that word as a "breath prayer" for twenty-four hours.

# VI.
# That Spring Should Vanish

*The death and resurrection of childhood*

"Alas," said Omar Kayyam, "that spring should
vanish like the rose, that youth's sweet scented
manuscript should close...." My childhood is dead, I
said; I can't bring it back to life. I grieved it, I let it go,
and I assumed it had gone to wherever childhood
goes when it dies.

And then I became a pilgrim to my own
childhood.

Fifty years ago I left Superior, Arizona. I was
eleven years old and I couldn't remember ever living
anywhere else. I learned all my values in Superior,
discovered how to be a friend and an enemy, learned
how to read and write. I went through spiritual
formation and learned the names of a hundred rocks
and a thousand desert plants.

Because of the novel I was writing, I went back
this year. Much of the town is boarded over. The
Magma—it was the deepest copper mine in the
United States and maybe the world when I lived
there—hadn't operated for years. Some of the houses

are abandoned, their windows covered with plywood. But a young woman at the Hamburger King was enthusiastic.

"The mine is working again," she said, deftly rolling a Green Burro. "People are coming home. Are you back to stay?" She looked at my silk shirt and my Birkenstocks and nodded hopefully.

"No, just for some hours," I told her as I wound up a roll of film I'd shot.

In 1942 I took a last look at Apache Leap, the rose-colored pinnacles that overlord all other mountains for five hundred miles and keep the town in its place; and Picket Post and the wine-colored rocky butte that looks like a buffalo, southwest of town, and the pale vermilion talings from Sam Herron's mine on the hill; and I got in the back seat of my parents' car with my dog, and we drove away. We had lived for several years on Magma Avenue, a big house with a basement and a giant palo verde tree in the back yard, and then in a Company house at the top of Copper Street.

My two old houses are both still intact; the brown stucco Company house is now painted white, with cypress trees funereal beside the porch. The present owner had invited me inside, to see the remodeling; but in spite of his having turned the big glassed-in porch that was my bedroom into many rooms, and in spite of his having added a new utility area and yellow appliances, the living room and kitchen were the same, and I took pictures of everything.

Something began to wriggle inside me.

A Company house was owned, of coursed, by Magma Mine Co., where my father worked. Most fathers worked at the mine, *if* they worked; some people's dads were out of jobs and they went on

Relief and their mothers did ironing. By the summer of 1942 when we left, the mine was on a wartime schedule and the Depression was over. On Copper Street the red brick houses—ours was the one stucco building—were for "straw bosses" and engineers and other men who wore ties to work. They still have big, gray, glassed-in wooden porches attached to the back that served as kids' bedrooms and utility areas.

"A lot is gone, isn't it?" the woman at the restaurant said, plunging a basket of French fries into hot oil.

"The skyline's the same," I said, beginning to tremble for no reason I could explain. I loaded a roll of slide film and went outside. I shot frame after frame of Apache Leap, where Geronimo's men are supposed to have ridden their horses off the mountain to avoid capture, and where, they say, you can sometimes see an immortal 400-year-old Spanish soldier, in helmet and armor, leading his horse through the pink pinnacles, still looking for the cities of gold. Big boys at school sometimes said they'd met the man up in the rocks, and talked to him in Spanish. White block-faulted limestone hills, full of fossils, front Apache Leap; Sam Herron's mine talings still lie red and permanent on the cactus-dotted slopes.

In the wintertime, those mountains sing. Cold winds forced through those rose-colored spires at high speeds sometimes create a high, clear call and sometimes deep tones like the notes of a pipe organ. We'd walk to school backwards, so the pebbles that bounced in the gale winds would strike our calves instead of our shins; and we'd sing along with the mountains. I swore I'd grow up and write an opera, using those pinnacle tones.

51

Pickett Post, on the west, looks like a man's classical profile. The red-to-blue rock formation rises behind the Boyce Thompson Arboretum, one of the finest collections of desert and arid-soil plants in the world. Our Girl Scout troop and groups from the Community Church had picnics there and then we followed Mr. Gibson, the ranger, through the park. Sometimes he gave us green pods, perfectly round with soft green spines: "Those are porcupine eggs," he'd say with his shy smile. He and his family lived at the old Thompson house that nestled well into its granite and sandstone environs. I remember falling down in that house while my parents played bridge with the Gibsons; and I thought as my head clanked against the pink flagstone that if I lived there, I'd pad those floors.

On the west end were Laster's Garage and the ice house. I won a footrace one July 4th, from Laster's to Seymour's Drugs. The distance looks pitiful now, but I was panting in the heat. Pat Gorham, the sheriff, gave me a silver dollar as first prize. Later, in high school and college, I became a record-breaking miler. I hadn't known, until that festival day, that I could run so fast.

In summer, we chased the ice wagon as it made its way up Magma Avenue. Sometimes the driver would give us a hunk of the sawdust-edged ice; sometimes we stole one. Serious entertainment and important ceremonies took place in Superior High School auditorium. The school is still standing; the dark red brick and the pillars are intact, through close to a hundred years' worth of graduations, magic shows, Tom Thumb weddings, Boy Scout Courts of Honor, and tap dance recitals. My mother was the town piano teacher; her recitals were either in our home or in the church basement.

The church is still standing, also, its gray stucco now white but otherwise much the same. I wondered if the basement still smelled of damp cement and coffee. But nobody was around, so I looked at the windows and remembered praying inside, remembered promising Jesus my whole heart.

I went back into the restaurant. "The smelter," I said. "The stack is cold and it looks so barren down there. Isn't it working?"

"They smelt down at San Manuel," the waitress said. "Magma owns that town, too." I closed my eyes and thought about the thick yellow smoke belching from that ancient brick stack; we weren't supposed to run or play hard in the late afternoon when the day's copper was being smelted and the heavy sulfur smoke billowed over the town. I can still taste it, remembering. The sulfuric acid bath leaches every last drop of copper from the ores: malachite, azurite, chalcopyrite, and rare bubble-topped copper dioptase. After sunset, when the smelting was done, the western rim of our world turned red and fiery as they poured the hot slag. The stack is about a hundred years old now. So am I.

We learned in Superior to live with death. Some of my friends' fathers died in the mine, crushed in a cave-in, or from silicosis of the lung—"rock-in-the-box," they called it—they'd picked up working in the mines in Colorado before they came to Superior. My friend Paul, who lived next door, came out one morning with his blue Swedish eyes bleached by pain. He was four; I was six.

"My Daddy went away last night," he said. I already knew; my mother had been called out after we were all in bed. I had heard Paul's mother, sobbing. They had come from Sweden together, Paul's parents. His older sister Berit yelled and threw things around the house all day, while Paul and I hammered a fort together in the yard.

On this trip I didn't find any of the wild burros that roamed the yards and hills and even the streets when I lived there. We threw our garbage in a small canyon behind the house and the burros ate it, paper and all. We watched them eat prickly pear cactus, too, the juice dripping down their thick donkey lips, and we wondered why the spines didn't injure them. The burros seemed not to feel it, or they took it as just one more sadness in their lives. They had tragic faces and necks, but we rarely pitied them because they were so cruel.

Our burros were ex-mining donkeys or descendants: Crippled Jack, Silver King—he was the meanest burro in Pinal County—Short Tail, Whiskey, Brown Boy, Lobo. I don't remember any females, but since the burros kept proliferating, we must have seen some. One morning we woke up in our house and found a burro inexplicably trapped in our service porch, braying to be heard across the world.

Climb on a burro that's been hanging around your back yard all day eating carrot peelings from your hand, and he'll head straight for a clothesline to scrape you off. Or he'll twist around and, with the same velvety mouth and square teeth, bite your foot. We used to rope those burros and ride them, and they usually bucked us off. One threw me clear up on the tin roof of that same service porch; I still bear a scar near my right elbow where the edge of the roof cut me.

I saw the shadow of ears, moving to shake off flies and gnats; I heard the thump, thump, thump, tha-dump of Crippled Jack, walking across the rocky yard.

Someone inside me whirled around and danced.

Scorpions, black widows, mean-biting tarantulas, Gila monsters and rattlesnakes were our only childhood enemies: human beings left us alone. Perhaps there were rapes and incests and molestations in our town, but I was never warned of any such danger. If I got lost in the hills, some miner would always point the way home for me.

I went to Roosevelt School. The red brick building is still there, and when I peered through the door window, the main hall looked the same. They've bricked in the windows, though, adding air conditioning and windows on the far side, and torn down the older gray stucco building where Miss Miller taught me to read in first grade, and Miss Knowles taught me to think in second. Miss Knowles was the first true professional teacher I knew; when I taught school years later, I heard her voice in my voice.

Once on the way to school we found a man dying in a ditch. At first we thought he was drunk, and we tittered; but he twitched and thrashed; his skin was turning blue and his chest bloomed with blood like a bouquet of carnations. Someone got Mr. Stone, our principal, and he shooed us away; but I memorized the man's face, his sensitive lips and wondering, confused eyes. He had dark hair and needed a shave. Later that day he died. A red-haired young teacher at our school whispered to us that he had shot himself after finding out his wife was in love with another man. We wondered later where the gun was, and why we hadn't seen it.

Most of our teachers lived at the red brick Hotel Magma. Miss Spain, the geography teacher, held Mineral Club groups there, in the genteel old lobby. She read the names of our mineral samples from a book: "Chalk-o-pyrite," she said, holding up a hunk of chalcopyrite, and we covered our mouths to be polite, not to laugh at her ignorance. She was from the east, after all, a florid, crepy-necked woman in her middle thirties, too smart to teach in a little place like Superior, but needing the job.

The turn-of-the-century inlay on the rusty exterior still says "Hotel Magma"; so does the inscription in the sidewalk. Now a sign at the lobby door says "Wing's Hotel."

The Wings and the Hings were really Ongs; we called our grocer Mr. Hing, but his daughter Lily, my schoolmate, explained that Ong Hing and Ong Wing were brothers, and that in China the last name came first. We could get penny candy and O Henry! surprise packs and movie tickets at Hing's while our mothers shopped for eggs at ten cents a dozen, or chose steaks and chops from the skylighted meat counter. We had to shake our shoes when we got outside, to remove the clinging damp sawdust.

In the fall of 1940, Spanish Flu swept through Superior. I had never seen my parents sick in bed before. On Thanksgiving Day they sent me to the restaurant side of the Silver Dollar; for fifty-five cents I had a huge traditional dinner, and for another dollar, I took a lunch pail full of turkey and dressing home to my parents. I was the only customer that afternoon, so two waitresses and the cook hovered over me, feeling desperately sorry for the

nine-year-old girl who had to eat in a cafe. But I was
having the time of my life. I'd never eaten alone in a
restaurant before, and I was thrilled. Apache Leap
glowed nearly crimson in the November sunset as I
walked home with the metal lunch bucket; my heart
was full.

When crossing Queen Creek to the south side of
town, kids turned their heads away from the stone
building on the bank of Queen Creek; we didn't
know why, but our mothers said not to look. Their
lips were set tight about that building. I found out
years later it was a small brothel; now, it's a bed and
breakfast, carefully restored.

I photographed boarded-up buildings: the
Uptown Theatre, Hing's, the drug stores. As I started
to step across Magma at Main, a flashing "Don't
Walk" signal held me on the empty street between
abandoned businesses.

I felt my childhood, living and whole, surge
inside me. I stood in line at the Uptown, waiting to
see *Suez* with Tyrone Power and Annabella. I drank
my first chocolate soda (on my knees so I could reach
the straw) at Seymour's drugstore, where, when the
red light was on over the door in the back, you knew
the pharmacist was developing film.

I was back in that church, not remembering this
time, but singing hymns and winning a
leatherette-covered Bible for selling the second
greatest number of religious pictures (a girl named
Letty Orr got the white Bible for selling even more
than I). There was no Episcopal church in Superior,
so our family attended the Community Church, the
one now painted white.

*I never put away* all *childish things*, I thought; I still
have that Bible, along with a number of other

translations. I read that Bible until pages fell out; I let the word of God dwell in me, I let the verses I memorized for Sunday school fall into the ground and split open and grow until I had a whole tree of Scripture in me. When I gave my whole heart to Jesus one summer afternoon as I sat on that hard pew, praying to be better than I was, I gave it forever: I never took it back.

*Unless you become as a little child....*

"Every time you opened your Bible, you did that," Jesus says.

Then childhood isn't dead; it's squirming inside me, demanding that I listen to its simplicity and gentleness. And somehow, as I stood in a street of boarded-up stores, I felt more alive, more absolved somehow, than I had for a long, long time.

"Come back soon," the woman at the restaurant said.

"Yes," I said, thinking about the book I was writing, thinking about the old stone brothel as a place to finish it. I left and stood on the bumper of my rental car to shoot another roll of the mountains, and then headed out into the forest of ancient saguaro and cholla, lacy mesquites with their fierce thorns and long curved pods, and the faithful palo verde that has erupted into bloom without fail, as soon as spring rains leap joyfully down the arroyos, maybe every year since Creation.

## For Reflection

Not everybody has the chance to go visit their hometown or old neighborhood; but you can always return in your mind—

not to bad times with your parents or days when you felt lost and alone, but to a day when you found a flower or played with your dog or fell in love with your teacher. Keeping youth alive acknowledges that God was always present in your life. And you'll recall fine stories to tell your children or other young friends.

## *For Faith-Sharing*

In a small group, recall the very best day in your childhood. Describe the physical setting in which you experienced that day. Discuss the ways God was active in your life on that day.

## *Prayer*

> *Thank you, God, for my childhood. Help me to recall and enjoy everything that was good, and to forgive those who hurt me or misused me. Let me be in such a state of grace that I can look back and see God's hand in all my life. Amen.*

## *Journaling Idea:*

Pretend you're a child again—say, eight years old or some other age you choose. Write a diary of an experience you remember, trying to be the child you were then.

# VII.
# The Beginning of Wisdom

*The fear of death, and the death of fear*

I stand in front of the mirror, trying to comprehend the fact that this body, albeit in pretty good shape, is more than sixty years old and that one day not too far hence I'll finally have fulfilled my wish to behold God face to face.

Death, our last enemy, waves at me from the mirror, from behind my own eyes, and I flinch.

In some societies at some times I would have been highly honored for my age. But now my younger friends think the greatest compliment they can offer is denial: the Demon is already activated in them. They try to reassure me by saying, "We would never guess you were over sixty, Kris. You're the youngest woman we know..."

They don't know how patronizing that sounds. Is sixty-three something ugly, that I should disguise it, deny it, betray it? As they speak, I recall a line in one of George MacDonald's fairy tales: "Of course I am old; am I not beautiful?" And I wonder if any of these unknowingly bigoted young women also insists to others, "Why, some of my best friends are sixty!"

An evil creature thrusts itself in to harass me. This demon hopes to reduce me to babyhood. She invented magazines with "Golden" in their titles, and she calls old women "Sweetie." The demon is dangerous because she invites me to see my aging not as a process of lost beauty, discovered wisdom, death, dust, and finally resurrection—but as an opportunity to become attractively childlike. The demon, a dumb spirit that loudly kids with and flirts with her elders, would rather rock a baby than try to manage a wise old woman. Many nursing home workers are afflicted by this demon, indwelt by its foolishness.

This isn't the worst of it. The demon's most destructive activity is Cute. Give me a few years and the demon-possessed will no longer say of me, activist or outspoken or strong: instead, they'll say I'm spry and peppery and willful (in fact, if I live long enough, I'll even be called cantankerous). My friend had been married nearly fifty years, then was a widow for ten more; then someone put her in touch with her high-school sweetheart, whose wife had also died. They married several months after their reunion, and the otherwise-sensible people around them began to coo and hum like idiots.

"Isn't that *cuuute!*" they crooned, in a tone one might use while leaning over a crib. "Aren't they adorable?"

It wasn't cute, and they weren't adorable; they were deeply in love, a couple who chose at nearly eighty to give themselves to that love. Like all married people, they experience physical pleasure and humor and an end to loneliness—along with jealousy and inconvenience and fighting over housekeeping or politics. These are dignified humans whose skills and wisdom should be recognized; but the demon, perhaps unable to stand the very thought of old bodies rubbing together in love or of white-haired folks quarreling like newlyweds, reduces them to Cute.

Even the people who run our local Senior Center are so chillingly patient and feloniously hearty that I avoid the place—actually, I try to avoid anyplace that calls me a Senior or any events with euphemistic names like Golden Opportunities. I don't need to be cheered up or cajoled or kidded; nor do I need some Thirtysomething with a fresh M.S.W. to devise time-killing education or entertainment for me.

These years, this seventh decade and beyond, aren't Senior or Golden or Adorable. They are simply the time that leads toward my end. And the physical process is hard.

Once I could run long distances like the wind; I could almost fly; I could press my bosom against the tape and hear the crowd cheer. Now my bones are brittling, and when I jogged around our neighborhood loop, I chipped my heel. My doctor shook her head and reminded me that at my age I needed lower-impact exercise.

Once I could play the piano better than anyone in town, I could rip out a Beethoven sonata or a Brahms intermezzo with ease and *elan*. Now my wrists ache and my fingers protest when they try to leap from octave to octave of Schumann or ornament Bach with an inverted trill.

Once I could read until dawn and still make it through the day; I could dance or talk all night; I could easily lift a laughing, twenty-pound infant over my head. Once I was straight as a birch tree, thin as a winter fox, blond as dawn. Now I go to bed earlier and still sleep less; my strength is subsiding. I have begun to bend in the wind of time, to fatten and slump with gravity, and my blondness relies on artifice.

I hate all these aging symptoms: must I wear out before I die? And must I die before I see God?

Wisdom whispers, Yes, that as I get closer to the end, Yes, I must become more infirm, more dependent on other people, more wakeful in the middle of the night, and more scared. Scared of senility, incontinence, pain—and most of all, scared of seeing God face to face, even though that has been what I have longed for all my life.

The concept of being in the Presence is glorious, the longing for it unassuageable, and the reality terrifying. What if God doesn't like me? What if I don't like God? What if I glance at the Throne and dissolve in awe until there's no trace of me?

Yet these fears of aging and death are the beginnings of power and glory and a new kind of humility. Once I danced heedless of time to the altar on Sunday mornings, to receive Communion; now I kneel with some terror as I take the Elements, because—at last—I realize what I am doing. Once I was smart; now I am wise as an ancient stone.

My teenage grandson, with his straight teeth and unscathed eyes is not afraid of death: he shoots over curbs and curves on his skateboard, helmetless, daring injury, believing he will be young and immune to serious pain forever. Neither is he yet wise. I was like that once.

But somewhere in the past ten years or so I began to see the terminus of the journey, and my bones shrank with fear of it; my marrow is drying and my eyes have lost focus for fear of it. The picture of myself as a crazed old woman with loose skin on my neck and arms, with raddled face and rheumy eye, lying in my own pee, finally having to experience that terrifying moment that means the end of mortality—this is scary stuff. So if I want to experience aging neither by becoming Cute, nor with existential despair, the only thing left for me is to let fear lead me to wisdom.

For the fears of old age are preparation, teaching me finally to hate this body until I am willing to depart from it, the way pubescent daughters despise their mothers for a while, to dull the pain of leaving and starting their own adult lives. This fear is the shaping of my spirit for death and resurrection; and as I begin to lean toward God with age, I cast out the demon of Cute and offer my earned wisdom to the world.

A few come to me already: my grandchildren, asking what is a runcible spoon, or how do you find gold, or what are Fibonacci numbers; young writers, burgeoning with talent and energy, begging to know how to calm that raw ability into strings of words that people want to read; friends whose spouses hit them or drink too much, and who long to know what to do; neighbors who inquire about how to rid the cat of hairballs or find a wall stud to hang a picture. Everyone I know in their forties wants to know when I finally made myself happy, and how they can do it, too.

And the more active my fear of dying ugly and insane, and the harder I quake at the thought of seeing God face to face, the wiser I get. Wisdom is a stop on the journey, an opportunity to share my

knowledge and anyone's hunger for it. Just as I had
to resurrect childhood within me, now I have to put
to death the fear of ending: and then I shall see God.

My friends might be right; maybe I don't look like
a sixty-three-year-old woman. I still wear Reeboks
and designer jeans, my ears are double-pierced, and I
like some wild music. But time has brought me to the
brink of old age, and pushed me in, and I must swim
madly toward death, then God, urged on by fear and
the other voices of wisdom that went before me.

## For Reflection

The onset of age can seem swifter than a change in weather:
one day you're twenty, the next forty, and then suddenly you
find yourself feeling young—but you're sixty-five years old.
How many people in your church community or at work
have you passed over as potential friends because they're
"too young" or "too old"? What do you know about the inner
lives of older people, including your parents or aging neighbors?

## For Faith-Sharing

Talk about your feelings about growing old. How do you
plan to overcome society's stereotypes? Try to include all
ages in your discussion: childhood, adolescence, young
adulthood, midlife, older adulthood. Exchange ideas about
the Church's role in ministering to people of all ages.

## Prayer

*Help me to face old age with more than resignation,
God, and allow me to form honest relationships with
people of all ages. Amen.*

## *Journaling Idea*

In six columns, write the names of friends in these age groups: twenty-five or younger, under forty-eight, between forty-nine and fifty-nine, between sixty and seventy, between seventy and eighty, eighty and older. Pick one friend from each column and write down the special qualities they contribute to your life.

# VIII.
# Between Betrayal and Glory

*The death and resurrection of God*

Humbly I adore thee, Verity unseen
Whom thy glory hidest neath these shadows mean
Lo, to Thee surrendered, my whole heart is bowed,
Tranced as it beholds Thee, shrinéd in the cloud.[1]

*Well, this is silly,* I thought as I got up from the kneeler. I was in the basement of the church, keeping my hour of the "watch" on Maundy Thursday.

It's an ancient tradition. After the Eucharist and foot-washing on Maundy Thursday, the altar is stripped, the frontals and superfrontals carried away, the Bible slammed shut and carried into the sacristy, and the Sacrament jerked from the tabernacle, whose doors are left flung open; and that Sacrament is removed to the Altar of Repose.

In some parishes this altar is decked with flowers (because Jesus prayed in a garden before he was betrayed, or maybe because he was eventually buried

---

[1]  The quoted texts throughout this story are attributed to St. Thomas Aquinas, 1225-1274.

in a garden tomb); in some, the altar is bare and solemn except for one candle and the Host, usually covered; at our parish, the altar guild creates Repose in the Children's Chapel, downstairs.

Our altar guild has a collection of white organza altar cloths, veils, and frontals. After these coverings are in place, they lay the Body of Christ on a silver paten on the children's altar, and cover it with a pyramided veil of white lace. Then they create a small aisle of candles on graduated tables and station a prie-dieu at the end of the aisle. The air is redolent with melted beeswax; the darkness in the rest of the room is thick and prepaschal.

We sign up for hour-long shifts to "watch" all night, to kneel or sit before the altar, to replace burned-down candles, because in Gethsemane Jesus said to his disciples, "Could you not watch with me one hour?"

No, they couldn't. No. The disciples couldn't watch, not for five minutes, the sight of Jesus falling on the ground, praying in despair, sweat falling off his forehead like clots. But now we know the end of the story; so we come in at eleven at night or 2 a.m. or whatever, enthusiastic for the task, cheeks busked with the night cold of early spring, bristling slightly with our own importance, and take our places, relieving the one who was most recently on duty. We bring rosaries, Jesus Prayer beads, icons, sometimes a devotional book, although it's hard to read even in so much candlelight.

Besides, how can you *watch* if you're reading? I could be caught up by some tricky point of theology and miss God passing by.

Not that I noticed God passing by as I crept into the Children's Chapel. I was in a fit of pique, sleepy and wondering if I had signed up for this pre-dawn hour to show off, or whether I really expected some miracle to occur.

> Taste and touch and Vision to discern Thee fail,
> Faith that comes by hearing pierces through the veil
> I believe whate'er the Son of God hath told:
> What the Truth hath spoken, that for truth I hold.

*This is silly*, I said, rising from the kneeler. I'd read the Collect for Purity and said some Our Fathers; now what was I going to do to keep busy for an hour? What had I done in all the previous years I'd been here?

I could hear footsteps overhead: two men were keeping a different kind of watch up there all night over the women and occasional man who showed up to serve at the altar of repose. We're a downtown church, and although this is not such a large city, we've had our share of rapes and robberies. So every year two or three men of our parish manifest their devotion to Christ and his Church by escorting people to and from the parking lot, by making sure nobody but Watchers slips through the door.

I couldn't remember feeling so restless on other Maundy Thursdays. Tired, sleepy, yes; sometimes the one hour went by awfully slowly. But this time I was downright irritable.

*Maybe the evangelicals are right*, I thought. *Maybe this is idolatry or foolishness.*

I glanced at the altar. The Body of Christ lay hidden in its swaths of white lace and organdy; the altar reminded me of nothing so much as a newborn's bassinet. That's the way we like Jesus: a baby, harmless and mild, sleeping beatifically. The minute he grows up and reveals himself as the universal Wild Man, we get scared, and nail him down to a cross so he can't interfere in our lives or be abrasive to society or trouble anybody. Of course, we soon discover that the *crucified* Christ is far more trouble to the world than the preaching one: first of all, there's that chancy business of redemption, and then the minute he dies, we're threatened with Resurrection.

I crept toward the altar and fingered the frontal; I wished that I could in all sincerity kiss the hem, or maybe even prostrate myself there. But I could see myself; I can almost always see myself, except when I'm taking photographs. My camera is complicated enough so that I can't think about one other thing when I'm lying on the forest floor, trying to keep my shutter open long enough to record a drop of tree sap on a mushroom, or when I'm thudding across the desert, bracketing exposure after exposure of the red mountains.

That's one of the reasons I love photography. When I take pictures, I'm relieved of the burden of observation (and judgment) of my own actions. The rest of the time I'm constantly aware of me.

So I can't be like the wonderful Armenian Orthodox woman we saw in Jerusalem, who placed kiss after tearful kiss on the altar cloth at the Church of the Holy Sepulchre. She was honest, absorbed in God; I would be alert to my audience—even if it were only me.

Maybe I'm denied this devotional life so that I'll seek the face of God in silence alone.

"But I need something visual, something tangible," I said, still standing by the altar. One of the candles guttered out, so I spent the next five minutes replacing soft stubs with tall, unused tapers. The fragrance of wax was almost overwhelming; merry shadows danced on the walls. *But this isn't exactly what I meant by something tangible,* I said. I sat down and began writing my complaints in my journal.

*How can Repose come before death?* I wrote. I mean, if you're acting out the story, is Jesus resting quietly somewhere, or is he being dragged through Jerusalem, into a kangaroo court and an illegal meeting of the Sanhedrin? How can he be in repose before he's even tried by Pilate? Am I watching a dead, pre- resurrection Christ, in the garden where he was buried, or am I watching his agony in the garden of Gethsemane? And if this is the Agony, why do we have him decked out in white lace? Why don't we have a hunk of granite here, instead of an altar? And why do we watch for about fourteen hours (until around 11:30 on Good Friday morning) instead of the *one* that he asked for?

*Why are we not watching against the devil?* I wrote. After all, before he went to the garden, he told his friends, "I won't talk long; the prince of this world is already on his way." Yes. Yes. It was the Wilderness all over again, only worse: this time Satan could point to God, could to Jesus call God the villain. "Ask him to take this away," the devil must have said. "Tell him you can't go through with it." Shouldn't the Watch include ordering the devil away from our Lord and off church property? Why, instead, am I encouraged to focus on myself and my own spirituality?

Feeling better now that I'd put my irritation into words—feeling, in fact, a little like Martin Luther—I wrote, *And why are we putting all this emphasis on individual, rather than corporate, devotion?* I mean, if there's anything the Church has taught me in the last twenty years or so, it's to believe in the worshiping community, the blessed company of all the faithful in perfect common-union with Christ. Isn't that the real power of the Church—corporate worship in the Eucharist? Then what was I doing here all alone, pretending to be holy?

And I wrote, *Aren't we holding ourselves as superior to the saints, to Christ's own chosen disciples?* After all, none of, or at least most of, the Eleven couldn't watch; maybe John did, because he recorded some spectacular words and events. John didn't run away, like the others; he slipped in to watch the trial before the Sanhedrin, he stood at the foot of the Cross, he took Mary to be his Mother. But the rest, Peter and James and the others—they couldn't bear it, they slipped into what St. Luke calls "the sleep of sorrow," the stupor of acute depression, unable to witness the agony of their Master. Then why should I assume the posture of superiority? Am I better than the chosen saints? Am I showing off to God, saying, "Look, all those others fell asleep, but here I am."

A candle flickered.

A candle flickered, changing the shadows on my notebook. I looked up out of my pool of self-indulgence to see if a window was up, exposed to the wet night breeze, or if perhaps someone had opened the door. But nothing else stirred; only a candle flickered, but the tiny alteration in the shadow had transformed the room.

*Watch,* Someone whispered in my head. *Watch, watch.* I held my breath: was Christ about to reveal himself?

Nothing moved; nobody came. My heart was scarcely beating. Almost without volition I rose and went to the altar and touched the veil over the Sacrament.

"I have to see," I said aloud, and lifted the veil. Sacrilege? I don't know; nobody ever mentioned looking or not looking. I know I only had to glimpse whatever or Whoever lay beneath the white lace.

The Host rested on the silver paten, its round whiteness gleaming in the candlelight. It was familiar, ordinary, as known as milk or white socks or beach stones, as everyday as Bread, as plain as the moon. I stared, transfixed, still holding the corner of the veil in my right hand.

> O memorial wondrous of the Lord's own death;
> living Bread that givest all thy creatures breath,
> grant my spirit ever by thy life may live,
> to my taste thy sweetness, never-failing, give.

*Watch, watch.* I replaced the veil and went to the kneeler where I could view the altar. The candles blazed like fiery angels; I watched the shadows change and change and change on the white altar coverings and within the veil. God was alive, God was in heaven and on the cross and in the house of Caiphas, God was healing the sick and creating the world and weeping in the garden. God was everywhere, everytime, and God lay beneath white lace in a form I'd known all my life.

I wanted to stay in that room forever; I wanted to hold that moment; I wanted to pray but could find no words; finally, I began to sing.

> Jesus, whom now hidden, I by faith behold;
> what my soul doth long for, that thy word foretold.
> Face to face thy splendor I at last shall see,
> In the vision glorious, blessed Lord, of thee.

## For Reflection

Why did Jesus ask his disciples to watch with him while he prayed in Gethsemane? Did he know beforehand that they would fall asleep? When you believe you have failed God, what do you pray? And what would you trade to see God, face to face?

## For Faith-Sharing

Exchange experiences of vigils before the Blessed Sacrament, late-night times of prayer and/or loneliness, rituals of betrayal. Discuss the ways God has "resurrected" you in those experiences.

## Prayer

> Lord Jesus, you ask that I watch with you. Give me
> the strength to stay awake, to be steadfast and
> unswerving, to face your enemies and mine with
> resolution but without rancor, and at the end, to see
> you face to face. Amen

## Journaling Idea

If you have an opportunity to "watch" at an Altar of Repose during Holy Week, journal your moment-by-moment reaction. If you don't have such an opportunity, keep a late-night vigil at any time of year, lighting a candle and writing down what God reveals to you about Resurrection.

# IX.
# Who Killed Stutz Bearcat?

*The death of an invented man, and
the resurrection of a real one*

When I was seventeen and he twenty-one,
Richard[1] and I met and fell in love and planned to
marry. But nine days before the wedding he asked to
have the wedding canceled forever.

I was heartbroken for a long time, and then and I
got married to someone else and Richard became
Stutz Bearcat, and Stutz was murdered.

When Richard was about seven, his father, an
elfin man with dancing eyes, bought a Stutz Bearcat
automobile, and kept it in the garage behind their
wrecking yard.

"Someday, Son, this will all be yours," lied the
kind little man who knew how to make the Bearcat
growl with pleasure as he set the timer and honed the
points; but *Someday Son* never came because a buyer
with cash took it away and Richard's father, Ike, went

---

[1] This is a real person with a made-up name to protect his
privacy.

back to finding bumpers and fenders for people, so he could earn money to hush his nagging wife.

Richard meanwhile fantasized a Happy Family wherein he would sit on his mother's lap and his father—grown tall and dignified— would strum a guitar; the four of them (his sister was present) would sing in harmony after which his father fondly said good night. His mother, with miraculous brown eyes and tender lips, would kneel to kiss him; his father's cocky gait and his mother's tiny, angry, iceblue hogeyes would be gone forever.

When Richard was in high school his father's wartime junk profits and successful bookie enterprises and God knows what else brought them to more money than they needed. They should have moved from the dark cavelike house behind the wrecking yard into a Happy Family home on a street with green lawns and bicycles. But instead there was a string of racing ponies and an eight-foot sloop.

Richard's mother grew more angry and bought his sister expensive clothes and sent her to modeling school; and Richard bought a Stutz Bearcat car in poor repair. In 1943 and 1944 he drove it to school, full of laughing girls who wore frizzy pompadours and short wartime skirts, until the middle of his eighteenth year when pain he didn't know he had made him collapse.

He fell in pain one day (and again when he was thirty); and when it happened for the third time at forty, he realized how many of his years had been an alcohol-pot-speed-cocaine-acid-blurred tapestry of running from pain. In high school he learned his spine was a discoid stack, a set of china plates placed atop one another; and some near the middle had pulled outward and cracked and been ruined, so he

lived for a while in greenwalled hospital rooms; and
in those days when laminectomies and fusions were
not routine and easy, he had cruel indignities
performed on his mind and body.

And while he was recovering, the Stutz was sold.

Three years later, Richard and I met in a college
class, and we fell in love (or at least I did) and by
midsummer we were engaged to get married. But
Richard grew dark and moody and chafed at the idea
of constant friendship and civility and monogamy;
and nine days before the wedding, with my silvery
taffeta dress hanging in my bedroom, he asked to
have the wedding canceled.

Twenty years after that, in the East Village of New
York, where Richard stood with his friends in a
basement tavern, a foreigner asked his name. The
foreigner was sincere: an English major from
somewhere, with his brand-new Phi Beta Kappa key
trembling at his watchpocket; and he came right to
where Richard had been murmuring some of his
poetry to a few friends, and asked his name.

That was in 1967, the Summer of Love, and for
Richard the second Shark summer. The first had
begun the year before in North Africa when,
swimming one night in the Bay of Tangiers, he heard
in the moonless dark the swishing of a Shark near
him; and he swam furiously for the raft. And the next
day, just after he had shipped another batch of heroin
to America, somebody shot at him in the narrow
street and missed and killed his friend Dion. And
Richard went home.

Tired and wounded by experience, he made his
way across the Atlantic and in New York, frightened
of both sides of the law, began calling himself
Jonathan Ruckleshouse and Jesse Hindskill and Billy

Malone. And then one day a foreigner, who might have been a CIA agent or a disaffected heroin dealer or just an English major, sidled up to Richard in the tavern where he was murmuring a few poems to his friends, and asked, "What is your name?"

Without hesitation, Richard replied, "Stutz Bearcat," and thus he who was conceived so long before was born.

His girl friend, Linnea, rubbed her dark head against his shoulder and trilled, "Stutz, baby, buy me another beer."

"Two drafts," Stutz Bearcat sang to the Ray, the purple-cheeked, acne-scarred barman, who answered easily, "Okay, Stutz." And Richard was never called by any other name in that place, or many other places, again. In fact, even after Stutz died, there were those who still called him that.

Stutz drank his draft with Linnea and tried to understand what the foreigner was saying: he was asking Straight questions into everyone's Trip. Everyone in Ray's was stoned, some up, some down, some in their pot (or acid) nine days old. And this clean-shaven straight foreigner was asking questions, trying through Stutz Bearcat to define the hip society that he so longed to join.

Richard's backache made him want to snarl at the intrusion, but newborn Stutz loved everyone over the dark red bridge of his pain, loved through the drugs and despair that lingered in the brain he had inherited from Richard; so he looked at the outsider, whose lips were moist with hope, his honor society key flashing like a salmon lure; and Stutz said, "I am a streetsinger."

Stutz Bearcat, born by the foreigner out of Ray's Tavern, his newborn body already ravaged by years of drugs and booze and carnal pursuit and pain, full of poems Richard could never have written, leapt onto a barstool to chant a poem, twenty years before the Rappers.

O that Stutzian poetry sung thereafter into the street and onto paper every night! Poems of incredible wonder and joy, poems addressed to Babyhippers and Hell's Angels and faces in windows, to girls he loved and girls who loved him; poems to be intoned into the Street Church of St. Maryjane of the Flowering Tops by its chief priest, Stutz Bearcat.

Stutz was not a "multiple personality." Neither was he mad, or possessed. Richard had chosen Stutz unknowingly as a small child, and had just now brought him into being.

And in time, he was properly clothed in fringed leathers and beaded vests, capes, flowing sleeves, peace signs and jeweled roach clips; once a pair of gray doeskin boots and once a plumed leather hat. Stutz Bearcat was elegant in his tight pants and gold shirt, a red chiffon scarf knotted at his throat (a secret garrote to foretell his sacrifice).

It was 1967; it was time; and Stutz, having sung his songs to New York for several months, set his face toward California. He took with him a gentle, trembling, dark-eyed girl named Jennifer Horn, and his eight-year-old son, issue of his earlier marriage; took him so his former wife, Dorothea, a wise-faced, solemn bank teller, could have a vacation.

Heading across the country in a plane, he glanced down at lakes and rivers far below and knew that the Shark Season was no longer restricted to summer. Across the American continent they were there, Sharks, waiting, like the one that had brushed his body in Tangiers a year before. He had read that Sharks' bodies were covered with taste buds: and a Shark had tasted him as he swam in the darkness, and now the Sharks of America were waiting for him. By the time the plane set down in LA, in an onshore breeze, the smell of Shark was so strong in his throat and nostrils that he added cocaine to the uppers and downers he swallowed in his morning orange juice.

Stutz headed for haunts Richard had known in the days when we were both young, and for the places he'd lived with Dorothea, and places where he'd taught school and written a textbook and been unfaithful. He sought his oldest lays: the Sunset Strip, Barney's Beanery, and Whiskey-A-Go-Go; he went to all the cities of Los Angeles, the beach towns and the movie towns, blessing and touching. It was Stutztime, and he was brother, father, uncle, son, and carnal relation to all who came.

"Streetsongs!" he'd cry, the pain in his back still a pale mouse in his brain, sorrow a spider in his shoe, knowledge of his own death imminent. He rode in triumph down the Strip not on a donkey but on a motorcycle, with Jennifer Horn behind him, her long dark hair streaming like a flag in the bright night. The sidewalks were crawling with the Sixties, with miniskirted models of great beauty, and high-breasted teenyboppers, runaway babies and prostitutes, woman and man, girl and boy; with angry draftable boys and tie-dyed hippy girls in pioneer boots, and forty-year-old Pretenders, embarrassing with their long gray hair and dark glasses: all these turned their love on Stutz in the metropolis where Everybody Must Get Stoned. Stoned Stutz who before he went to North Africa had written an English textbook and sired a son and had edited an anthology. Now he filled his mouth and nose and veins with pills and granules and blotter paper, and he became mayor of the great city where everyone was stoned.

He went to Venice, California, where the once-elegant ballrooms were empty and falling into the sea when Stutz got there; once when I was seventeen, Richard and I had danced all night at a ballroom in Venice, so that my gold kid slippers were worn clear through, so at dawn he carried me, laughing gently across our damp front lawn to my father's door.

Venice had never been able to shift from Beatnik to Hippie days; Stutz stood on the beach and wept for Tyre, Sidon, Capernaum, Venice, condemned cities. Bag ladies sat on benches in the afternoon, looking into the sea, and young Caucasians in saffron with Asiatic pigtails, to be heavenhoist, handed out incense. They still read poetry with bongos in Venice, they were unready for Stutz; the faithful there believed Kerouac would return off the road.

One night at a crumbling Venice bar, where a few dull-eyed jazz musicians in black leather jackets listened to Streetsongs, Jennifer Horn said, "Stutz, I want to go."

"Sure, Baby. Where to? Back to the Strip?"

"I mean I want to go home. To New York."

And then they insisted, Jennifer and Richard's son, that he buy a Hippie van with curtains and brown blankets, lined with carpet scraps; and though he protested that he was a forty-year-old with a backache, not a Flower Child, he sold his motorcycle and he and his son Martin, not quite nine, and Jennifer, whose hair fell on the tops of her arms like a cape, drove and camped across the country; and it was because he loved them.

By now it was the summer of 1968 and while all over America grown men and women went to jail with young boys and girls because they were angry about the war and the dope laws and the government, the three travelers camped near lakes and ponds and rivers. Nervous, patient Jennifer and nine-year-old Martin watched as Stutz tried to enter lake after lake and stream after stream. They watched Stutz Bearcat, savior of poets and potsmokers, trying over and over to get past the edge of the water, afraid to swim out to where rain and melted snow had—he was certain—produced monster Sharks with double rows of three-foot teeth. And over and over he explained to Martin, who said there were no sharks in fresh water, that a shark was not the same as a Shark.

They drove down endless back roads and at night they rolled Stutz into a sleeping bag while he wailed that the clear night air was wrong for his city lungs; but Jennifer and Martin thrived under the trees. Jennifer cooked their dinners at night at the very edge of lakes where he knew pre-Cambrian eyes waited to seek out his blood. He insisted the Sharks retracted their dorsal fins and hid in alpine lakewaters, lay on the sandy bottoms of rivers in red canyons; and in spite of encouraging cries and the fact the young Martin swam and dived like a dolphin all around him, he couldn't swim into the water.

One night he tried while they were asleep, but failed, and came back wet and trembling, and smoked a joint for comfort but found none; and he fell asleep and dreamed he was in the water, swimming for his life, and was torn apart by sharp teeth; and his own screaming woke him. When he woke it was to the kindly, trembling hand of Jennifer, who stroked his brow and kissed his eyelids to give him better dreams.

And in that moment of Shark-eaten terror, he murmured, "I love you, Jennifer." At that very moment, Stutz knew his days were numbered; he felt life ebbing away.

Three days later they were married in a small town in Wyoming, and they sold the van and flew back to LA to open the old house where Richard had lived with Dorothea. They bought bean-bag chairs and paisley spreads, and tried to be a Happy Family; but it was too late, Stutz Bearcat was dead and Richard was not alive to love. After only eight months Jennifer left, weeping and sorry, her belongings in two cardboard boxes and a suitcase. Stutz sold the house and sent Martin back to his mother.

I met him by accident a few years later. I was visiting a daughter in California, recovering from divorce and a too-soon-after divorce romance that had ended badly. I went to cash a check in a bank, and there he was. We said each others' names aloud and laughed, and people turned to look; so we finished our bank business and went to drink wine and eat dinner in his spare, penitent apartment that still overlooked his old Sunset Strip haunts.

Richard was still handsome, although his cheeks showed grief and his back was slashed by the scars of six surgeries. He was forty-four, with beautiful lips and penitent eyes, trying, like so many, to undo the effects of LSD and alcohol and pot with crunchy granola and vitamin capsules, inedible wooden bread and raw honey and yogurt, offering meditation and

Dickens in the evening and a menial job all as reconciliation to his body and environment.

"You look just the same," he said, and I said, "I look forty-one. But you haven't changed," and we laughed again and went off to eat lunch, to eat dinner, to sit on the balcony of his apartment and talk. We talked for thirty hours.

I mean we drank tea and wine and water and more tea, we stood outside, we sat inside, we stretched on the floor and stared at his embossed tin ceiling, we walked around the block, we ate from time to time, but we never slept, not in thirty hours. I told him  I had married and mothered and gone to school, had quit writing and given ten thousand piano lessons, living for more than twenty years in a marriage so bad I don't know how we emerged alive. And he told me about Stutz Bearcat.

"Murderer, murderer," I said. "Tell me the truth: how did he die? Did you kill him with your little bow and arrow?"

"He died of repetition," Richard told me, thin and exhausted.

"Murderer!" I insisted. "You wanted Jennifer for yourself, so you killed him."

"Perhaps he died of a thousand overdoses," Richard pleaded. "We took a lot of drugs in those days. Or maybe a Shark ate him, that night he had the terrible dream."

"Never," I said, "never. You killed him. Why?"

"I swear, I loved him, I fed him, I kept him out of the water, I gave him my textbook royalties. Perhaps he was martyred for the people who loved him, perhaps he was taken directly into heaven."

"You killed him," I said, but suddenly my conviction weakened, for I sensed the presence of something that began as a tingle in my fingers and traveled to the right corner of my brain, something that was not I nor Richard nor Stutz Bearcat no any other earthly person: it was Christ.

Something loud as the words of creation rang in me and echoed and echoed and echoed. A great tower of bells began to peal inside me as if I were tuned to a certain oscillation and the right note would shatter my conscious mind; and Christ had sounded it. Stars began to fall around me, and the angels who, in ebullient glory, drive those stars swooshed by my head like joyful bats in a lavender twilight; and Richard said again, "I didn't kill him."

"I know," I said.

"But—"

"Yes, I thought you murdered him, to have Jennifer for yourself, or maybe fought with him in passion and accidentally slew him, or smothered him when your back went bad and Jennifer left. But I was wrong."

"Who, then?" Richard asked.

I took a deep breath to cram my lungs full of air and maybe the Holy Spirit, and I said, "Well."

"Well? Who did it?"

As slowly as I could say only one word, I said, "God."

"Are you crazy? What had God to gain from the death of...of an invented man?"

"You," I said. "And you better prepare yourself because he's going to kill you, too. Christ is on the move."

"Nonsense!" Richard said and for a moment I remembered how when I was seventeen and he twenty-one, we once argued the meaning of a line of Shakespeare; he'd cried "Nonsense!" that time, too, and we grew so passionate, so sure of our rightness, that we flew at each other scratching and biting and yanking until one of us laughed and we fell to my mother's carpet, laughing and kissing.

"I thought Christ was the victim, not the killer," Richard said, and then I told him about the times I had tried suicide and failed, but how I'd gotten so good at it that after that long, last coma from overdose, Christ knew he might lose me, knew I might make it the next time, knew I had to be killed so I could live.

We sat in that apartment on the hill overlooking Sunset Strip, looking out at the banana-tree fronds combing the surface of the swimming pool; and in spite of Richard's books on astrology and the I Ching, I knew the patchouli incense rising from the brass burner was really owning Christ as deity nigh. We were sipping papaya-mint tea, which I dislike but not so much as the Turkish coffee he'd made; there I sat in my eighty-dollar jeans (which look just like the cheap ones), with the long blond hair he remembered now short and expensive: a grown woman with grown children and eyeglasses for the astigmatism all musicians seem to get.

Only an hour before, we'd been remembering how we used to drive to school in his ancient Ford; now here I was in his post-hippy Sunset Strip apartment, saying that Christ was a killer and he might as well prepare to die.

"But I know God in my way," he said, pointing around the room at his books and symbols.

"Those are pictures about God," I said. "Come on, put your head in the lion's mouth."

"What makes you think God wants to kill me?"

"Who killed Stutz Bearcat?" I asked.

86

Christ, the great Consumer. He wouldn't take the suicidal little scrap of self I offered him; no, he had to keep on until I was skinned out and hanging up and infused with eternal life. And now Richard was marked for execution, too.

You've seen it in the movies.

Two Mafiosi catch each other's eye at a dance. One breaks away from his beautiful partner and goes to plant a kiss full on the mouth of the other man.

"Gino, you're a dead man," the kisser says with a macabre smile, and the other clutches his breast in terror, knowing that his days are numbered, that he will live now looking over his shoulder, waiting for the sight of an oiled gun muzzle pointed at his head.

"Stutz, Richard, whoever you are, you're a dead man," I told him. "Christ has marked you for reaping, for burning alive, for stuffing into the insatiable maw of his heart. It's a terrible thing to fall into the hands of the living God; don't be fooled by his frequent appearances as a baby in the manger, or as a fool on the Cross."

"But why, then?" Richard begged. "If God wants me, then why kill the part that was giving and good?"

"Stutz was a fake," I said. "Maya. A man of Gomorrah. He only seemed good because he didn't have to be real. You loved the best of yourself in Stutz, just as I once fell in love with the primordial Stutz in you."

"Nonsense!" he roared, but it was the hollow roar of a toothless beast. He began to weaken; he let me open the Bible he had tucked between the *Bhagvad-Gita* and *The Mystery of the Pyramids*.

He strayed to the Gospel of St. John, and he paled and flinched and looked over his shoulder, and he let his finger rest on the line.

"Is this true?" he whispered, pointing to the testament of the disciple, holding his hand over words that might deliver him from thousands of nights' wallowing in drugs, from the burden of Streetsongs and the blood-guilt of Stutz Bearcat.

"Do you believe this?" he cried. "Do you think it's true?"

*Gra'mother? Is this like Santa Claus?*

The name and sorrow of Stutz Bearcat disappeared from my sight; Richard's sin teetered on the edge of forgiveness; a seraphim with a hot coal hovered overhead; myriad, myriad angels held their breath.

"It's true," I said, and I told him everything, beginning with death and then what comes afterward.

## For Reflection

The author of this book has laid open her own identity as well as that of her friend Stutz Bearcat. How often do you reveal yourself to the world? Are there times when it's appropriate to hide behind some mask, even if that mask is merely social convention? What would happen in a world where everyone was transparent and truthful all the time? Would that lead to chaos, or would it bring about the Kingdom of God?

## For Faith-Sharing

If you lived through the sex-drugs-rock-n-roll ethos of the Sixties, discuss how that era has affected your life today. If you were not born or too young to be aware of what was happening, talk about the residual effects you think you see in the Church and the world. Tell one another about at least one mask each of you wear in society and how it separates you from God and other human beings.

## *Prayer*

*Christ, your death and resurrection are all around
me. Help me to kill the "false self" I sometimes
become and the masks I wear to avoid your presence.
Amen.*

## *Journaling Idea*

Not too many of us are as complex as Richard/Stutz Bearcat, but we all have identities and behaviors we take refuge in. In your journal, list the ways you show the world an unreal self and name the reasons you think you do it. Then, write a description of the real you and how God pursues that identity.

# Epilogue

"Your brother will rise again," Jesus assured her. "I know he will rise again," Martha replied, "in the resurrection on the last day." Jesus told her, "I am the resurrection and the life..." (Jn 11:24-25 RSV).

Behold, I tell you a mystery: we shall not all sleep, but we shall all be changed, in a moment, in the twinkling of an eye, at the last trumpet... (1 Cor 15:51).

Life isn't just something Christ brought to earth; life is something Christ *is*. He is truly alive, and is life; is resurrected and is The Resurrection. Without him was no thing made; without him will no thing live at the end.

Christ's thumbprint is all over creation, reminding us of the fact that although death is present, he has overcome it and we can overcome it through him. But first we have to submit, to drink the cup he drained, to drag our crosses through the streets, to be willing to fall into the tomb so he can raise us up. And this is the great mystery, revealed for all time: that we shall all be changed, for better or for worse, into something eternal.